MW00609835

WAR STORIES
& REMEMBRANCE

The Extraordinary Stories of The Ordinary
Men and Women of the 20th Century

WAR STORIES
& REMEMBRANCE

The Extraordinary Stories of The Ordinary Men and Women of the 20th Century

General Editor: Rev. John P. Cardamone Sr., M.Div.
Co-Editor: Micah James Cardamone, B.A.

LibertyNewsPublishing.com
PO Box 943
South Norwalk, CT 06856
Email All materials & Photos to: Revjohnnycardamone@gmail.com
OFFICE: 203-838-0100

Copyright © 2020 by Rev. John P. Cardamone Sr.

All rights reserved. This book may not be reproduced in whole or in part without written permission from the author; except by a reviewer who may quote brief passages in review; nor may any part of this book be reproduced, stored in a retrieval system, or transmitted in any form or by any means, electronic, mechanical, photocopying, recording, or other, without written permission from the author.

LIBERTYNEWSPUBLISHING.COM
PO Box 943
South Norwalk, CT 06856
OFFICE: 203-838-0100---E-mail: Revjohnnycardamone@gmail.com

Designed by: Pat Creedon Design, Inc.
Cover Design: Pat Creedon Design, Inc.

Library of Congress Control Number: 2020942341

ISBN: 978-1-7353838-0-4

ACKNOWLEDGMENT

There are many to acknowledge who had to live with me or at least put up with me during these years and especially past months to complete this project which began in 1994. Indulge me to give them the recognition they so deserve:

First to my family; My lovely wife of 30 years, the former Miss Jill Marie Gentry, and our four boys John-Philip Jr., Luke Daniel, Micah James, & Isaiah 'Boo Boo' Gentry. They have endured ME and should all get a medal!

An old friend Lorrain Duncan; she got me in touch with Valerie Utton, who became my Publishing Coach and motivator; and Pat Creedon Design, Inc. for my cover, photo editing and formatting.

My late Grandmother, Mary Cardamone and my four WWII veteran uncles Frank, Carl, Tony, & Bucky.

My godfather Dom 'CUZ' Cardamone, an Army veteran, who calls me 'Pastor Pro' and is a veteran and Always believed in this project, and when I was about to abandon it many years ago, said to me, 'You have to finish it!'

To Stew Leonard who without knowing it directly, provided much motivation from a sign I saw at his offices back in 2008 when I visited the HR person Chris Arnette for some support with our local Calf Pasture beach 'Revival Fest'. The sign over her door read;

'SUCCESS COMES TO THE FEW WHO FOCUS IN AND FOLLOW THROUGH.'

Those words have kept me on track through many difficult days, weeks, months, and years of distraction.

To my third son Micah, who served as co-editor and who laboriously typed the manuscript from the taped interviews. I told him often, 'If it were easy it would already be done!'

To my Father Dominick, pictured on the back cover, who was also an Army veteran and died in May of the COVID-19 alone in a nursing home here in Connecticut. He called me 'The Professor' when I was a just a kid with a big mouth who liked to talk. I guess I haven't changed much!

To my late mother, Anna Marino Cardamone who Always believed in me, and raised me to be a Patriot. I'd like to think she would be proud of my humble efforts.

And to GOD who has Always been my best friend, and source of inspiration.

And finally, to the many veterans and family members who opened their lives and hearts to share and remember these Stories. I hope the reader feels a bit like going through a family scrapbook. Though some memories are often painful, the hope is that we may forever appreciate the great sacrifices they made. Some have asked me; Why are you bothering to go through all the trouble, expense, aggravation to even write this book? I would like to think it is so that we may express our eternal gratitude for the gift of freedom these have purchased on our behalf, that we may enjoy and cherish our wonderful Liberty!

Rev. J.P.C., July 15, 2020

TABLE OF CONTENTS:

INTRODUCTION

War affects all of our lives and has throughout the history of mankind struggle for meaning and existence. The severity of its impact was perhaps most heartbreakingly felt in the 20th Century with four major wars taking the lives of more than 100 million souls from numerous countries and changing the political global landscape of our world forever.

Every human being who has lived through the history of such horrors is impacted and changed; their lives, never to be the same again. And the way they approach life and its story is forever shaded and molded by these events.

There is much to learn from these 'War Stories' and experiences, be they military or civilian. And so, we attempt to give voice to these individuals and events, with three focuses in mind.

First, to remember the history. It has been said that, 'Those who forget the past, are destined to repeat it!' And with that, all its costly mistakes.

Second, to honor the sacrifices of those courageous, brave soldiers who gave of themselves and to us, 'the last full measure of devotion,' that we might know the great Liberty their blood has secured for ourselves.

And third, to strive to prevent future wars. It has been said the first casualty of war is The Truth. We hope that is a small way this book could inspire others to share their stories and experiences to pass on to the next generation, that those priceless lessons in history, may never be forgotten.

Rev. J.P.C., June 30, 2020

PREFACE

At the outset let me say, I am not a United States military veteran. I joined "God's Army" in August 1977, the week that Elvis Presley died, coincidently who was an Army veteran. I headed south with some friends to Hollywood Florida to attend Florida Bible College for the next 5 years. And after that three more years in the Washington DC area at Capital Bible Seminary, M.Div. 1988, I have pastored three churches in Connecticut.

The title for this book came to me in 1994. But the inspiration for this project and book, I guess you could say grew from my childhood curiosity, having four uncles who served in WWII. As kids we grew up playing army with my brothers and the boys in the neighborhood. Everybody wanted to be on my side because I had 'The Bazooka Blaster' and our sub-machine guns. But my mother taught us, never to point a gun at anybody!

In 1984 I saw then President Reagan give his stirring address in Normandy France on the 40th anniversary of D-Day. He later went to a war cemetery in Bitburg Germany which caused some controversy due to the fact that it held SS remains of former Nazi soldiers.

I traveled to Europe the following Summer of 1985 with a seminary buddy, and out of curiosity, we tracked down the same cemetery we had seen in I believe a Time magazine article and the S.S. grave. I spent nine adventurous weeks visiting 15 different countries all over Eastern and Western Europe!

Among them we visited the site of a famous WWI battlefield in France, and three former communist countries which no longer exist, including East Berlin and Check point Charlie. I got lost from my three buddies coming out of a museum, and somehow, I don't recall seeing the Brandenburg Gate! But I still remember the fear on the faces of the people of East Berlin, as they cautiously pointed the way to help me return to West Berlin. On to Czechoslovakia and Prague, which in spite of having many buildings still in a state of disrepair, was among the most beautiful cities of Europe with its stunning Baroque architecture. The Russians were still there 'celebrating' 40 years of 'liberation.' Of course they had entered in 1968 to crush student rebellion. In 1985 we met Jiri 'Georgie' on the street and he allowed Tommy & I to stayed in his little flat on Lazarska Street for four nights. I remember shopping on a Saturday morning in a large supermarket in Prague, packed with people. And when we got to the meat aisle there was a large long open deep freezer, with one piece of green meat sitting on the bottom. That was a powerful illustration to me of the drawbacks of the communist system which squashed free enterprise. All that has now changed.

I'd like to think between our friendship and encouragement and Bruce Springsteen's album that summer 'Born in the USA' we played a small role in the 'Velvet Revolution' which began November 17, 1989 as Jiri helped lead the student protests for change, from which eventually emerged a Free Czech Republic.

I also visited what was at the time Yugoslavia, (Actually Croatia though I was not sure where I was). Someone in Italy said go see Dubrovnik! So, I took the boat from Bari Italy one night, slept on the outside deck and arrived in the morning to Beautiful Dubrovnik! It was prior to the civil war which would engulf and divide the country in 1992 along ethnic and religious lines exposing the tensions that had simmered under the surface for decades but which Tito with his strong arm had been able to keep in check. At that time his picture and portrait still hung in nearly every home, tavern, or store, over the doorway.

And then on to the island of Split to see the Europeans enjoying themselves on summer holidays and then to the capital of Zagreb. I met wonderful people all along the way who just wanted to be free to enjoy their lives in peace. And wherever we went the Europeans treated us with kindness and respect, and I sensed an underlying appreciation for Americas help in saving their countries on two occasions in both World Wars. And I suppose America was in a way returning the favor for especially the help of France in our own Revolution for Independence in 1776. Of course, not All Europeans share the joy celebrated in American Liberty. I did not realize that till years later when several British friends were leaving the country for holiday around this time of year. (July 1 at writing) Then it dawned on me why their distaste for the American 4th of July. They lost the war!

Well then on to Bastogne Belgium to a memorial commemorating American General McAuliffe's reply of 'Nuts' to the Germans request of surrender, before he and his besieged troops were rescued by General Patton's Third Army. And then to beautiful Luxembourg where we visited the grave of General George Patton whom my uncle Bucky Tavella fought with in the 3rd Armor division.

Later, during my first pastorate in June 6, 1994 I was painting my grandmothers living room. She had just been diagnosed with cancer and died that November 24th at the age of 90. On that day as we watched the ceremony at Normandy, I asked her to tell me stories about the war and living through the Depression. Having been born in 1904 she had lived through many events in the 20th century.

Unfortunately, the tape being old and brittle, broke years later when I went to play it. That has served as a metaphor for the urgency and focus of this project, to record and preserve the history, and to honor the sacrifices made on behalf of our great country.

The following year Tom Brokow came out with his best seller, "*The Greatest Generation*" and the race was on! (Oliver North also used the title **War Stories** in his 2003 book series) People began to realize the importance of recording the history regarding these more than 14 million great American patriots who had answered the call of duty and quietly and humbly served our country and who then had begun to die at a pace of 1000 per day. Now in 2020 we are losing the Last Voices of the War. I have heard it said by veterans that America does not ask or take territory from those we conquer in war, but only requests enough land to bury our fallen dead.

Now 25 years later the youngest remaining veterans of WWII are nearly 95 and so the task of collecting and preserving the stories falls to the children & grandchild. And not just stories of battle, but the stories of the home front and all the far-reaching ramifications of War and its effect upon our families.

Think about this; some of the greatest movies ever made, are in fact WAR STORIES!

GONE WITH THE WIND, IT'S A WONDERFUL LIFE, BEN HUR, LAWRENCE OF ARABIA,

FOR WHOM THE BELL TOLLS, SHINDLERS LIST, DIARY OF ANNE FRANK, And of Course, my personal favorite, CASABLANCA!

And so, we stop and consider WAR and how it touches each of us in profound and no doubt immeasurable ways.

We are living in anguished times of angst and of protest; In the midst of a global pandemic over COVID-19 and racial upheaval in "BLACK LIVES MATTER" movement, and protests of Indigenous People's claims, that are forcing America to face and ask many difficult questions with seemingly no easy answers. As we complete this project, we have been especially reminded of the vulnerability of our elderly veteran population. Recently in Holyoke, Massachusetts June 24, 2020, and all over the country, there has been a criminal amount of death of Veterans at nursing homes due to COVID-19. This has been repeated tragically in many states across our country; a travesty for which there must be some accountability to right this tremendous wrong.

There is something else that has often bothered me. And that is the TV campaigns and commercials that have become so common, pleading for monthly donations, often by celebrities, for veterans and tugging, as it were on our heart strings. Using little children and the sound of a sad tinny piano in the background is enough to make anyone open their wallets!

Without mentioning specific organizations, this author does not approve of this! I have no doubt there is some good these groups may well be accomplishing on behalf of our veterans. But in my mind, when a veteran returns home, especially wounded, with visible or the invisible scars from battle (This obvious mental health crisis is especially evident demonstrated by the high suicide rates among our veterans of the past several years), these returning veterans should receive a medical Cart-Blanche! Whatever they need, they get! Physical and mental health services must be readily available either through the VA hospital administration or use of Any and All public and private hospitals. And politicians would need that to be taken into serious consideration when formulating a Total Cost defense budget before they choose to send our brave men and women to war.

And let's remember to express our appreciation for these immeasurable sacrifices, in what has become a popular cliché perhaps, 'Thank you for your service.' And may we remember to never forget!

About the Cannon in the Cover photo.

Below each plaque of the names of those who served reads:
"WE HONOR THOSE WHO DO US HONOR."

The cannon pictured here was for many years at the local VFW on Cross street in Norwalk Connecticut. But several years ago, when the VFW closed it was repaired and restored and placed back on its original pedestal on the town Green. It was a French cannon used in WWI, captured by the German Army, and then recaptured by the French Army. It was presented to the city of Norwalk on July 16, 1921 by the Republic of France, as a gift for our help in the Allied Victory of what was called the Great War, WWI.

Here in New England where I was born and still live, we have a Town Green which in earlier Colonial times was the center and soul of a village or town. It is usually surrounded by churches marking the spiritual heart of a community. And there are usually placed there monuments, often War Memorials of some kind. They serve as a reminder of the price of our Liberty and express the gratitude and great debt of a free people.

The banner on this church, Black Lives Matter, illustrates at the time of this writing, the ongoing debate about righting our past wrongs, atonement for the sins of our fathers, and bringing justice and peace to those who have been long denied. All this is part of Americans effort to form what we call, a more perfect union.

The plaque reads:

'This monument is erected as a tribute of honor to the citizens of Norwalk, Conn., who devoted themselves to the causes of Freedom in service of our country during the Great World War 1917-1919.

And as a memorial to the men who made the Supreme sacrifice.'

There are 44 men from Norwalk listed who died serving our country in WWI.

Chapter 1

WORLD WAR I-1914-1918

Foreword & Introduction

The cost of war is often measured in blood and treasure. WWI had more than 70 million mobilized combatants, 60 million in Europe alone making it one of the largest and deadliest in history: The United States lost an estimated 116,000 soldiers. Total estimated 9 million soldiers and 13 million civilians killed. And the following 1918 Spanish flu influenza pandemic causing upwards of 50-100 million more deaths around the globe. (See Wikipedia)

World War One (WWI) was referred to as 'The Great War' and 'The War to End All Wars.' Perhaps because of the scale of destruction it shocked the supposedly civilized world, when the Industrial Revolution met with the advances in modern technology to mass produce the high capacity killing weapons such as the machine gun, mustard gas, armored tanks, long range artillery, the submarine, and great dreadnought battleships of many nations.

What started over the assassination of Archduke Franz Ferdinand in 1914 in the city of Sarajevo, grew to a global conflict that most especially ravaged the continent of Western Europe, lasting four grueling years until the Armistice of November 11, 1918. The resulting

Treaty of Versailles, lay the groundwork and ultimately the seeds that germinated into World War Two (WWII). (See the chapter, Origins of War, by Luke Cardamone).

Regrettably at time of publishing we have extremely limited story material in this chapter. Perhaps for some obvious reasons. I recently found several taped interviews from 1999, one in which I interviewed a women Pauline who was 100 at the time and shared some stories of her brothers who fought in the war. She died the following year. Today you will see within several of the stories from this book family members who mention fathers, and uncles who fought in WWI, but often with little information or recollection.

I interviewed a fellow in a local nursing home a couple years back and saw his notebook of his father's letters from WWI. We last spoke this past February seeking to use some of the material. But then once the COVID virus broke out in March, nursing home access and in person interviews became impossible. And sadly, in May as I attempted to gather my final material, I was informed that Bruce had died. As of today, I have not able to reach any family or find out what happened to the letters.

These types of events which happen all too often have added a renewed sense of urgency to complete this project. As I have shared for these past several years with many folks I have met or briefly interviewed, I pleaded with them, 'Write your story! Leave something behind for your grandchildren to remember and to know what you lived through!'

I realize in the end, these are personal decisions, that every individual must make. But if in a small way this book may motivate and accomplish that vision, I believe our families and our history will be the richer for it.

Rev. Johnny Cardamone
June 25, 2020

Edgar Taylor

WAR AND LIFE MEMORIES: A LASTING TRIBUTE:

This chapter on World War One (WWI) is our only story. This particular story as told by Bud Taylor about his uncle Lieutenant Edgar Taylor, USS Navy & 79th squadron RAF, (Royal Canadian Air Force) WWI, MIA, 1897-1918.

Photos and story as told by Bayden P. 'BUD' TAYLOR nephew, used with permission

Edgar's nephew 'Bud' son of his younger brother Bayden, shared some of the stories and family oral recollections of his uncle Edgar, one day over lunch at a local diner.

The story takes us from the wild range of his boyhood upbringing in Camas Meadows Idaho, to the US Navy, the Canadian RAF for flight training, and on to England, and eventually in the earliest days of what would be called, aerial combat, and finally in 1918, to the "Bloody Flanders Fields" of France, on the German Western front of WWI, where Lieutenant Edgar would meet his final fate. We are permitted only this glimpse for now of this one life from what was called 'The Great War.'

Born of courageous immigrant parents, who would raise four boys on what was then the rugged and wild American Western frontier; the life of the Taylor family is a story that should be told, and taken to heart for it is the truest stuff of American pioneering spirit and grit. Though the descriptions at times seeming almost mythical, courage embodied the lives of our great patriots and pioneers. In his letters he shares the parallel to knights of a former time to describe the chivalry these pilots afforded to one another, friend and foe alike.

We can only offer here this brief explanation of Edgar's final flight. He was shot down near the border of Germany and last seen by a fellow Allied pilot waving on the ground and disappearing into the woods, never to be heard from again. He would be listed as MIA; (Missing in Action).

Years later the family would attend a spiritualist church and hear the speaker acting as some sort of medium, who offered a type of 'word of knowledge' explanation by saying, that he believed Edgar was killed by a German farmer while stealing food. His remains have never been recovered.

And so, we offer what was considered among his mother's most treasured memento, his final citation:

'He whom this scroll commemorates was numbered among those who, at the call of King and Country, left all that was dear to them, endured hardness, faced dangers, and finally passed out of sight of men by the path of duty and self-sacrifice, giving up their own lives that others might live in freedom.

Let those who come after, see to it that his name be not forgotten.'

Lieut. Edgar Taylor

79th Squadron, Royal Air Force

Edgar Taylor, 1917, in the U.S. Navy

Uncle Edgar Age 18

Family War Photo of Edgar Taylor

PRIVY PURSE OFFICE.
BUCKINGHAM PALACE. S.W.

25th January, 1921.

Dear Madam,

The King and Queen have during the War invariably sent messages of sympathy to the nearest relative of those who have lost their lives in the service of their Country.

In cases of doubt, however, Their Majesties have refrained from sending any message, always hoping that the report might not be true.

The King and Queen have now heard with deep regret that the death of your son, Lieutenant E. Taylor, is presumed to have taken place in 1918, and I am commanded to convey to you the expression of Their Majesties' sympathy with you in your sorrow, and to assure you that during the long months of uncertainty Their Majesties' thoughts have been constantly with you and those who have been called upon to endure this exceptional burden of anxiety.

Yours very truly,

[signature]

Keeper of the Privy Purse.

Letter of Condolences

Bud continues his own family life stories, photos, and family recollections after WWI, in his own words.

My paternal grandfather, Peter Taylor and his brother Harry left England and came to America to homestead in the state of Idaho. My father, Bayden the youngest of the four brothers, left Idaho and came east to go to high school and then onto college. He had not been back to Idaho so in 1935 when he was married, he gathered up my mom, sister and I as family and decided it was time to visit what family remained in the home state. We drove west in a 1933 Ford, and although I was only four at the time, my fifth birthday was coming up in a few months. I recall a good deal of the trip, enough to know that flat tires were a regular occurrence, but in those days every driver carried patch kits to repair a hole in the inner tube as well as a hand pump to blow the tire up after repairs were made.

One sight I remember was going through the Black Hills and seeing Mt. Rushmore, and though it was a long time before it would officially open, I believe it was only George Washington's head visible at the time, people were able to watch the progress from the main road. It was VERY hot in S. Dakota and I recall dad buying a wash basin and some large blocks of ice to make an early, rudimentary AC for my sister and I! He kept it on the floor of the rear seat, which worked surprisingly well!

I also vividly remember him telling us that even though the Indian wars were pretty much a thing of the past, but that his uncle Harry had been in an altercation with an Indian and was struck in the jaw with a tomahawk leaving his left side jaw pretty disfigured. I also remember him warning my sister and I not to stare at uncle Harry's wound. Well, you know how it is if you tell a kid not to look at something! When we were there a short while, I couldn't take my eyes off uncle Harry, and found myself being scolded by the man himself, something like "if you keep staring at me, you might wind up with a same injury!" I think I wet my pants after that!

This was the first meeting with the "Idaho" family, and at this time only my dad and his younger brother were there. Dad had two older brothers Alfred and Edgar who left Idaho to join the military.

Uncle Alfred went to Canada and joined the Royal Flying Corps (later to become the RAF), while Edgar joined the US Navy with the stipulation he would get to be a pilot in the newly formed Navy Air Corps. After going through basic training and not being assigned to the Air corps, he went through the chain of command, all the way to the Secretary of the Navy, was granted an honorable discharge, and he too went to Canada and joined the RFC.

Alfred preceded his brother Edgar to fly in Europe and was shot down behind enemy lines, was captured and spent the remainder of the was in a German prison camp. He did survive and went on to become a noted cancer researcher at the University of Texas in Austin. While he didn't talk too much about the war, I do remember him telling me that there was little to do in his cell, that he trained cockroaches to do various tricks, and I was about ten years old at this point and fully believed him. As I grew older (and somewhat wiser) I began to question the fact, but unfortunately never saw him again, so I will believe he was jostling me, but who knows?

My next visit with the Idaho branch of the family came when I was 14 years old. My dad worked for the NYNH and Hartford RR (Rail Road) and was able to get passes from any other RR in the country, so he thought it would be good for me to travel from our home in Connecticut to Idaho, the only part he was required to pay was for my Pullman berth. The first leg of my journey took me to St. Louis where I meet up with my Cousin Duane (the son of Alfred) who was going to med school at Barnes Hospital in St. Louis. We spent a wonderful day, visited the St. Louis zoo, had a lunch and dinner and early evening I was back on the train to Idaho.

It was awhile before the conductor came around collecting tickets, and he informed me that passes were not recognized on the particular train and that I would have to disembark in Kansas City. I'm not sure if it was KC Kansas or KC Missouri, but they are side by side. I called my Uncle in Idaho to tell him what had happened and that I had made new arrangements and would leave later that evening. I thought it to be a grand adventure and was not upset about what happened, but when my uncle called my dad, I guess dad was so upset with what the conductor did to a lad traveling alone that he called the RR involved (the Southern Pacific) and ultimately the conductor was fired. I guess in this day and age it is hard for people to believe that a parent would let a 14-year-old travel that far alone, but I thought it was a GREAT experience.

Obviously I never met uncle Edgar as he also was shot down behind enemy lines landed safely as his fellow pilots followed him down and watched him climb out of the plane, wave to his fellow pilots, and was never seen again.

My grandmother Esther raised her four sons and a daughter here in this cabin. When it caught fire one day while she was visiting her neighbor, because the kids were playing with matches, all my grandfather could save was the sewing machine. Even after my grandfather had died at age 44 of Typhoid fever, and she lost my uncle Edgar in the war, and with little money she still persevered, and saw her three remaining sons through college. She remains to me a lifelong inspiration of true American grit, perseverance, and courage.

Life in Camas Meadows, 1910

Family Log Cabin which burned down.

Bud Taylor in Norwalk Connecticut, July 2020.

Bud also shared, a book which included letters, flying logs, and the diary of his uncle Edgar *"It's A Long Way to Camas Meadows."* Self -Published and edited by his late uncle Alfred E. Taylor and William 'Bud' Davis, by Idaho State University Press, Pocatello, Idaho, 1976. Alfred was also a WWI pilot who was shot down and became a POW (Prisoner of War). All four brothers were brilliant men, and Alfred went on to become a professor.

EDITOR'S NOTE: Bud also shared this story about a vacation several years ago to the French Virgin islands of Guadeloupe. While at dinner with his wife and another American couple, they were sharing a large table with six French speaking guests. Toward the end of the meal one of the Frenchman got up and said, 'As a tourist you would think when coming to a French territory you would attempt to speak the language!' To which his American friend replied; 'I visited Paris many years ago, and when I entered the city with my buddies, the people were in the streets cheering, and hugging and kissing us, and I don't recall any of them asking if we spoke French!' It was August 1944. Needless to say this particular Frenchman walked away without saying a word. It was of course the occasion of the Allied liberation of Paris from the Nazis.

Another antidote this editor recalls was years ago after the war I believe the Olympic committees were meeting. And one Frenchman complained, 'Why must we speak English at these meetings?' To which an Englishman replied, "I suppose it is because a few years ago we saw to it that you did not have to speak German!' Touché!

WWII-1938-1945

Foreword & Introduction

The cost of War. WWII is considered the deadliest conflict in human history with an estimated 70-85 million fatalities (see Wikipedia).

The main body of this book and its original inspiration is centered around those people, soldiers and civilians who lived through WWII. When I pastored my first church in Georgetown, CT in the 1990's we would hold a monthly veteran's breakfast on Saturday mornings. I loved to hear the men share their stories with one another. Guys would say their name and where they served and anything else they wanted to share. One day as we went around the room, one fellow said his name, and then said, 'Omaha Beach, that's about it.' That was the Most understated comment I had ever heard as Omaha was one of the bloodiest battles of WWII. But it illustrated to me how difficult it must be for a veteran to open themselves up to these memories.

We have divided this chapter into these two sections; Civilian and Military. At the writing of this we are celebrating the 75th anniversary of the end of what is referred to as 'The War'. The reader will find 'war overlap' as some individuals stories cover several wars. I challenge the reader today to look around you! The time is short and many of the remaining WWII vets are between 95-100 years of age. We are witnessing these last living chapters of history come to a close. Talk to your neighbors! Perhaps a bit difficult in these pandemic days but wear a mask and take time to listen to and to preserve these last living voices of history and their stories.

Rev. J.P.C.
July 26, 2020

Section A:
ANONYMOUS CIVILIAN STORIES

FOREWORD TO CIVILIAN WAR STORIES:

The following story is by and about civilians who lived through the horrors and heart ache of WWII. We have heard many others. But several individuals still could not commit to have their names being publicly associated with the horrors they faced, at least at this time. There are accounts of German soldiers who would go into Italian villages and rape the young girls forcing their parents to watch. And yet another German soldier who assisted an Italian girl who was trying to save the life of her mother.

For the Jews of Europe, the terror began in Germany after Kristallnacht AKA, the Night of Broken Glass (November 9-10, 1938 when Jewish businesses throughout Germany were, smashed, looted and ransacked, see Wikipedia). When the Germans entered Hungary in their march to Russia, I was told they would take Jewish men and march them ahead of the advancing armies in order to detect mine fields. Of course, many civilians died this way. And even if they managed to escape for a time, they would most likely end up in a place like Dachau concentration camp.

The Nazi Pogrom caused many Jews to try to flee Germany as refugees. The Nazis even had what was called 'The Madagascar Plan'. A proposal to deport and relocate the much of the Jewish population to the island of Madagascar (See Wikipedia). But because the plan became unfeasible and the fact that so very few countries took the Jews as refugees, so began the Holocaust or what the Nazi's referred to as 'The Final Solution'. The creation of mass concentration camps for the purpose of exterminating the Eastern European Jewish race which in the end took the lives of six million Jews, and many other individuals.

One country which did open its doors to Jews was the Philippines. Many Jews fled there and were treated fairly well by the Japanese initially. But near the wars end, as the Americans closed in and the Japanese recognized they were losing, they too committed the atrocities of rape and murder of many civilians.

The stories civilians have shared with me trace their journeys from places like Italy, Hungary, Russia, and Germany and eventually, on to a new life in the USA. They involve the life of Jews and the pain of Anti-Semitism. Others remind us that not All enemies are completely evil, thus illustrating the complexities of human nature even during war.

I want to share a brief story from my childhood about a German man named Albert and his daughter who years ago worked at CR Gibson with my father and lived here in town. It was near Christmas of circa 1965, and my parents took myself and my two brothers for a visit to their little home down the street. Before we went inside, I remember my parents specifically instructed us to greet them with, 'HAPPY HOLIDAYS" instead of 'MERRY CHRISTMAS' which we would normally do as Italian Catholics. No reason was given. I didn't realize it then, but no doubt they were Jewish, and survivors of a concentration camp who came to the US as refugees. I can recall the numbers tattooed on his forearm. We debate such things today, searching for political correctness, or Not! In that moment I would like to think that in a small way were practicing what Cary Grant as Dudley the Angel in the 1940 film 'The Bishops' Wife' called Christian charity, and tolerance, perhaps something that maybe in short supply today.

The irony is that after 75 years since the end of WWII, many people behind these stories and remembrances, still asked to be anonymous, or to not have their stories published at all. Perhaps to remind us that the reach and pull of history upon their lives remains a powerful one, and in some ways the ghosts of the past never fully leave us, and the soul scars of fear remain.

And in the words of my late Grandma who inspired the writing of this book, 'There is good and bad in every group!' In other words don't allow yourself to be prejudiced; to be racist; to be a bigot; to judge people by where someone comes from or what they look like; but rather, in your own little corner of the world, to listen, to extend a heart of compassion and as the Good Book says, to 'love your neighbor as yourself.'

Rev. J.P.C.

From Hungary: Journey to America

The story, is also done Anonymously in an interview format, as are others in the book, with questions or comments by the editor in (PARENTHESIS).

I was born in 1936, in Szekler in Hungary. My father was a landowner and also owned a business in the city. When he was young, he was considered a great looking guy and one day at the local swimming pool he met a swimmer, a beautiful young lady and they fell in love and soon after that got married. Well, my father was almost kicked out of the family because this beautiful woman was Jewish! And she naturally turned Catholic you know and joined the church. And brought my brother who was six years older, and myself up Catholic. That was considered an excessively big, horrible thing, that my father married a Jewish girl. But I think it was a beautiful love story, naturally.

So, this is how the horror story what I am telling you about the War is preceded by this very fact that she was Jewish. So, in 1944 the Germans troops moved physically, into Hungary. They came to my town and they called it S_____ ; they came in and then slowly investigated everybody. Fortunately, as I told you my mother was Catholic back then; they were looking for the Jews. But naturally deep down all the people knew that whether she was Jewish or not, the fact was going to eventually come out and very soon!

And sad to say her parents, and three sisters, they all died in the Holocaust, at Auschwitz. This was unbelievably bad and sad fact. All except, one brother, he somehow managed to survive and came back home! His name was 'Peter'.

So, by 1944 the German's, thank God, were losing the war, and the Russian's were coming into Hungary! By then my father was the head of the Fire Department in town. Everybody now fled from the Russians!

(Did you Hungarians get along with the Germans?)

Oh yes, of course. So anyway, we also had to run away from the Russians.

So, my father packed us into this great big fire truck and then we were heading toward Austria from the town of Szekler. And we arrived in Gyor Szent in Hungary. We were going toward Austria, but we did not get there, we just ended up at Gyor Szent and that is when the Russians moved upon us. So, we could not flee any further. And there my father was almost executed by the Russians because they found out we came from Szekler. That city was a very horrible city to the Russians because they had attempted to come in and the German soldiers were holding them back. The Russians again launched an offensive and again attempted to come in and the Germans pushed them back. There had been real street fighting!

So therefore, when the Russian's found out that we were from Szekler, that horrible place where they had got beaten twice, they said, "Ah you bastard," and they were ready to kill him the poor guy. And fortunately, there was a very nice Russian officer who also spoke German. So, my father was able to speak with him and he said, "Come on! I'm a fireman I had nothing to do with the fighting."

(Your father wasn't in the Military?)

Oh no, he was head of the Fire Department, the Fire Chief.

So finally, the man said, "Well I can't let you just go so easy." So, he said, I will shoot and then you lie down, and you pretend that I shot you. And he went behind a building, and he did that and then the Russian's left.

So, my father came back and as I told you, we were there waiting with the firetruck. My mother, my brother, myself and my father had taken all the gold and everything of value that we possessed from the house in Szekler. We had taken it with us, so naturally the Russian's got that from us! They cleaned us out completely! So, with only the little bit of money we had left was merely enough to buy a two-wheel carriage and an old horse.

This is the most important part of the story. After the Russians finally had left, and we were going to go back to our hometown with our two-wheel carriage and our horse. Just a little buggy, one horse, one lovely horse, and my brother; there were the four of us. So, we got back to Gyor, and from Gyor to Szent, we were going back to Szekler back to our hometown. It's about 80 miles, and we arrived to the main city of Gyor, and there were the Russian's again and they took away our horse! I guess horses were in demand for their army. So, there we were my family again with a two-wheel carriage and no horse.

We had to stay there for just for one day. That one-day delay will prove very significant. Then my father, finally bought another old horse for a flask bottle of rum! Just an old flask of rum. So, okay we lost a day right there. Now we got the little horse and we started to go back home. We arrived at the next village and we did not see anybody; all was incredibly quiet; we could feel something was horribly and totally wrong. And then finally, one of the peasants came out from hiding in a barn and told us what had happened yesterday.

The Russian soldiers came into town and raped the women you know, as sadly often happened in war time. Well one farmer came back, no doubt to exact for vengeance or retribution for that awful crime came and hit a Russian soldier in the head with an axe, which of course killed him. And so, for retaliation the Russian soldiers killed everybody, in the village! How tragic this was! But now you understand, if we did not lose the first horse, we would have been in the village the same day when this terrible event happened.

So, this is the most significant story in my life really. So that now if I am late for some engagement for whatever reason, it means God has something different in mind for me. God just saved me; you know. Therefore, I'm not in a hurry, I'm not in a hurry anywhere or anymore.

(What was the relation between Roman Catholics and Protestant in Hungary?)

It's just like here, meaning we had Reformadash (Reformed Protestant Christians). My best friend was J. P. he was a Reformadash. We also had Catholics, Evangelicals, and Jewish, and Greek Orthodox.. We did not have all the different denominations you see today.

(Everybody got along?) Oh absolutely, absolutely.

(How did the anti-Semitism begin? Did Hungary have a lot of Jewish people?)

We had the average number of Jews like most of Europe.

(Why did Hungary side with Germany?)

They were part of the Austrian Hapsburg Empire, (also known as the Austro-Hungarian Empire a dual monarchy and great power of Central Europe from 1867-1918; See Wikipedia) so of course, therefore we were with the Germans, that's where the national division was and always has been, geographically and culturally. For the before the Turks came in it was the Huns, it was always the Hungarian Austrian border that is how far everybody got (invading countries through the centuries), including the Russians, you see.

(So, you were like a buffer for Germany?)

Always, yes and that is why I really don't want to be bitter, but I have held animosity toward Hungary for national decisions that it has made. It was just a cesspool. Well, for example, my uncle who was an architect, he was also a card-carrying Nazi.

(What made them embrace Nazism, what was the attraction?)

They hated the Jews.

(Why did they hate the Jews?)

Well, I tell you I think it was centuries old, deep rooted. It was just looking down on Jews.

(But they were highly successful?)

Yeah maybe that is why they hated the Jews so much.

(That is why when your father married a Jew it was a scandal?)

Wow, what a scandal yeah.

(But your family was Catholic?)

Yeah, yes of course.

(How did her Jewish family feel about her becoming Catholic?)

I never, really knew. For example, in my hometown we had seven Catholic churches and we did have the gorgeous synagogue with the star of David and the Onion Dome. And sadly, that was torn down in 1944, when the Germans came in; they tore down the synagogue and then the Jews were deported. But first, the Nazis made the Jews to walk around with the yellow star, the yellow star of David, and then they disappeared. They were taken up immediately, within a couple days, and gone.

(Do you remember Kristallnacht?)

No, I was only three years old. But yes, that is how it started out all over the countries. My Jewish grandfather had a lovely ice cream and bakery shop.

(Were you very close to your grandfather?)

Not as much, well mostly my grandmother. Oh, they were gorgeous people.

(Did they make their own ice cream and everything?)

Everything, everything all homemade!

(I wish I had a picture. Did you ever watch the movie, "The Shop Around the Corner?)

Yes, of course, yes, yes just like that!

But, to understand even the closest family member my own uncle, had stolen oriental rugs, treasures, everything from the Jewish people. Everybody stole all their stuff! So, when anybody tells you that the Germans were sort of oblivious of what was going on with the Jews, that is a bunch of bullshit. The people knew and they were very happy about it. Because they got what the Jews had, so they were happy.

(So, are these people supposed to be Christians, Catholics?)

Catholic, everything, everything yes.

(Were there any priests that stood up?)

No, no, not that I recall.

(EDITOR'S NOTE: Dietrich Bonhoeffer was a German Lutheran priest who preached against Nazism and was executed in a German prison. They hung him with piano wire. He is best known for his classic book, "*The Cost of Discipleship*." See Wikipedia)

My education started with Nuns from grades one to four, and then I went to the Jesuits. Because you know my mother agreed that the kids, be brought up receiving Catholic education.

(Your escape sounds similar to the Von Trapp family in movie *'The Sound of Music'*?)

Yes, of course, yes! As I was telling you my father was taking us with the firetruck. But before that he had learned that already, people began suspecting my mother (To be Jewish). Before my father took us in the firetruck, we were already in hiding. My brother, myself, and my mother the three of us, were hiding already in the village of

Heviz. At Heviz, my father had this business of chimney cleaning. So, one of his helper's 'Henry', took us into his home and said that we were his family. So, I was going to school and saying my name was H----. He also was Catholic. And he continued to work for my father. He was claiming that he's the husband and my mother was the wife! Of course, this was to protect us and he just took us there to be in a safe place.

(He didn't have any family himself?)

Yes, sure he just transported us there and that is where we were hiding for a couple of days.

(So, you stayed in his house?)

Totally, strange house.

(As in the movie *"The Hiding Place"* or *"The Diary of Anne Frank?"*)

Well, in Heviz we were hiding out; absolutely. We stayed inside. So, that was the war years' experience.

(What about when the war ended where were you?)

Well, when the war ended, and the Russians came in and that was it. Then the Russians took over the country. They took away my father's farm, destroyed our gorgeous big house in my hometown. It was destroyed by what was called a *Stalin Organ*, which was an enormous missile! It hit the house and completely destroyed it! This occurred when we were gone and fleeing for our lives. Upon returning that's when we discovered that the house had been destroyed; the house was completely gone.

(How did you all manage to survive during those years?)

We lived very, very meagerly, we were totally poor, nearly starving.

(Did you have to work?)

Oh no, no my brother was in school. Father stayed as a fireman.

(What was your diet like?)

Lots of vegetables and no meat, no meat at all. Well, for a while we had the farm you know and then once the Russians came in, they confiscated it as I said, and it was all gone.

(What about the 1956 Hungarian uprising?)

When we finally got back from Szekler it was1956. That was the best part, totally the best part. You see in 1956 I was politically considered a non-desirable by the communist regime because of my father's background.

(And your mother?)

No, no, by then my mother issue of being Jewish was done; there was no problem. That is why my memories are not very fond of Hungary, to say the least, because of the way my mother's family was treated. Then the Russians turned around and gave us trouble because of my father because he was considered a wealthy man! Because the communists did not tolerate or live with wealth; the wealthy people were considered the enemy of the state in their Socialist system and way of thinking.

So, that 1956 was the most gorgeous time because there was the uprising against the Russians. And as I said, I was not able to go to college because we were discriminated against because of my father's background. So, I had to become a cabinet maker, a worker.

(They denied you college education?)

Yeah, the communists did. That was how it was. So, I became a wood worker,

(Did you go to a trade school instead?)

No, no I was a cabinet maker, apprentice. And after two years of work under a carpenter, I became a full-fledged cabinet maker, meaning I was a skilled worker. And then I was accepted in the academy of applied arts in Hungary, as a worker you understand. A worker is okay in communist society; an aristocrat is not okay. So, in October 1956 I went to the academy, it was all because of my cabinet maker background. I was asked to be in charge with the cabinet maker for the children (younger students), for their class instruction and learning.

And then, thank God, on the 23rd of October the Hungarian Revolution broke out and that was it! (EDITOR'S NOTE: It began, like most revolutions of our time, Including Tiananmen Square in 1989, and the Honk Kong protests of 2019, as a student led revolt. It was the first uprising against Soviet rule in Eastern Europe. Eventually over 200,000 Hungarians would flee the country as refugees, See Wikipedia).

So, from October 23rd until November 22nd my brother and I were in danger again. So, on the 22nd of November we crossed the border at the River Endau, under machine gun fire! The Russians were shooting at us!

(Did you have a boat?)

No, no it was a small stream we were able to wade across. They made a movie out of it with Yule Brenner, the River Endau. I fled into Austria; we were just telling ourselves, let's go leave this lousy country! That is how we felt then.

(So, you had become bitter towards Hungary, but now you were bitter toward the Russians?)

Well, sad to say, we came to really hate the Russians for the atheistic communist government they imposed upon us. But as life would have it, I ended up married to one! My wife is half Russian! So that is how life is, you just never know where fate will take us.

(Alright, so you flee into Austria?)

Yeah, and thank God for that because Tanta M---- was a S--- girl. Anyway, Tanta means "aunt," so Tanta M----, she was married to Uncle M-----, who was the general director of the Austrian Steel company. So, she and all other society ladies picked us up and we were carried around like the poor Hungarian refugees. They got Rockefeller scholarships for me, in Vienna. Academic for Applied Arts for me, which was a Rockefeller scholarship. And my brother did the Academy of Building and Fine Art as an architect. So, I finished up schooling in 1959, in Vienna. My brother the same. And we headed to America; he went to Los Angeles and I came to New York City. And we thought we would never look back to the lousy memories of Hungary again. But naturally, later as time passed, and wounds heal, we went back, and we stayed with my mother and father, and visited them.

I married my first wife in 1964 in New York city. She was Italian, and in 1969 our little daughter was born, and we were able to buy a fantastic house, carriage house in Connecticut. I fixed that house up and then sold it and we moved to another home. Then, unfortunately we got divorced, and she returned to New York.

In 1984, I met my second wife and we have lived here in this house since then.

From Russia with Love: Journey to America

My father actually drove for General Patton! When I was born, he got a telegram in Krinkelt, Belgium where he was stationed. He got the notice while in a foxhole that I was born! That was just before the war ended in 1945.

My grandparents also have a remarkably interesting story. They told me that they escaped during the Russian Revolution. And my mother was born in Turkey on the way over to Europe as they had to flee Russia in 1917. They were white Russians (EDITOR'S NOTE: A loose confederation of anti-communist forces who largely supported the Czar Nicholas II, and fought against the Bolsheviks known as the 'REDS' until WWII, See Wikipedia) One day the Bolsheviks came to their house and said, "Okay you can leave now." So, my grandparents had to pack up and leave immediately at gunpoint! In anticipation they had buried all their jewels because they knew almost certainly that this was coming. They buried everything in the back yard, and nobody ever found it. Later on, they went back and found it!

So, they escaped, and I don't know the name of the ship that they were on, but my grandmother was pregnant. They traveled on the Volga river. My grandmother gave birth to my mother who was born in Istanbul, Turkey on the way over to the United States. When they came to the United States they landed near Virginia. And my grandfather had been in the Cossacks army, a type of calvary, and he was an excellent horseback rider for his regiment and wore a smart looking uniform.

And so, he was a riding instructor and made his way north and he ended up being a riding instructor at the local horse-riding club. There he met someone who was a stockbroker. And my grandfather left the riding instructing job and became a stockbroker on Wall Street. And my grandmother was a French teacher and she lived in northern Virginia for a long time; She taught at one of the private schools down there. Anyway, that is my tale!

Section B: MILITARY STORIES

Army, Army Air Corp, Navy, Marines, Coast Guard and Merchant Marines

FOREWORD:

Though Europe had been at war since September 1, 1939 with Germany's invasion of Poland, for America WWII began in earnest on December 7, 1941 with the Japanese surprise and unprovoked attack on Pearl Harbor, Oahu, Hawaii. As FDR (President Franklin Delano Roosevelt) called it in his next day famous radio address, *'A day which will live in infamy.'* Perhaps no ship recalls the horrors of destruction wrecked upon the lives of innocent and unsuspecting American sailors that day than that of the USS Arizona. Today at Pearl Harbor there is a beautiful memorial built over where she and the remains of over 1,100 of her lost crew lie in rest. With Europe and parts of Asia now already fighting more than two years, America was forced to confront this threat head on. Many veterans I have heard from said they felt it was there duty to go down and enlist, and many did, literally by the millions! Here are some of their stories.

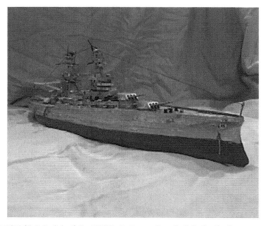

EDITOR'S Model of the USS Arizona battleship built for my sons

Part 1-ARMY

Andrew Mantlick: Europe

DATE ENLISTED & BRANCH OF SERVICE: WWII US ARMY 1942 to 1945.

THE WAR:

I was born in a village in the northeast part of Hungary. My parents immigrated when I was a young boy, like so many other Hungarians looking for the promise of opportunity that American provided. They settled in Norwalk, Connecticut where there was a large Hungarian community and many factories for work. It was the end of Depression time when the war broke out. My father had just started building this brick home where I still live! But you could not get any building material for private homes. Metal, copper, sugar everything was rationed, for the war effort you know.

As I look back to the war, the Japanese attacked us at Pearl Harbor in December 1941. When Germany attacked Poland two years earlier in 1939, I felt sorry for those poor people. The Germans had the Stuka dive bombers they go straight down nearly 400 miles an hour strafing and killing all the civilians. Anything that was under them they would bomb. Hundreds and thousands of Poland's people got killed on the first two days of war. It was terrible. I would have liked to go to Hungary where I was born, but I never got the chance.

LIFE IN THE INFANTRY:

Prior to going overseas, we first went to Massachusetts for our induction; we were there for a short while. There they told us if you have money or anything hide it in your pillow or some place, because they are going to steal your money! Then on to Texas for basic training. Now when you are in the Army, you do not go to a hotel and sleep in a nice bed; you sleep on the ground! You could find a nice rock for yourself, you used that as a pillow. When you were tired believe me you slept on it, you slept on a rock! We did not have sleeping bags; they gave you a blanket and a half of a pub tent. Two men got together and put two pup tents together and slept in the pup tent. Sometimes because it was raining you had to sleep in the mud or rain, you had no choice. You're in the army now boy!

BASIC TRAINING: SAN ANTONIO, TEXAS: SOME FUNNY MEMORIES:

Well there was a silly thing that happened one time we were bid wag (Camping out). You and the guys go someplace, and they stop to rest or something. We were in Texas (outside San Antonio) and it was kind of in a place with a lot of shrub bushes, there were no trees like around here, in Connecticut. Small as we are, I think we have more trees than all of Texas! And so, a lot of shrub and a lot of dry sand, and bugs too. Anyway, we were bedded down in open space and these dead looking shrub things were all over the place. Because you could turn it like this, and it breaks. It dried out but it's alive.

So anyway, we're sleeping one night, and I bid wag one night. It was quite bright, there was a bright moon that night. Before I fell asleep, I heard this rustling, and I said what the heck is that rustling. So maybe the 'enemy' (These were army drills) filtered into our position or one of their scouts was on our campsite. So, I hollered right away "Corporal of the guard, Corporal of the guard!" Calling the Corporal to check out what is going on what's making the noise. Corporal did not come so I start hollering "Sergeant of the guard, Sergeant of the guard!" So, he runs over to me and says what's going on. I said I heard something rustling in the bushes over here. He says what did you hear? I said, Well out there somewhere 20-30 feet from me. So, he says, you heard something? Well you know what that was? That was an armadillo walking around out there! An Armadillo! So, everybody laughed! They were ripping me after that for weeks after that, "Oh Andy saved the company from the enemy!" So, I was a hero, I saved the company from the enemy Armadillo!

HEADING OVERSEAS:

We finally were heading overseas in 1944. The United States had just built, a year or two before that, a cruise liner, and I think the name of it was the West Point. It was a 500-footer! When we came back after the war, we were on an old trap-steamer. I think going to Europe there were about 9,000 of us going over. Guys were sleeping all over on the deck and in the lower levels. We were right above the water line. All the big shots like generals and things were on the next floor. It was quiet; we did not have any submarines with us, for protection but the Germans had submarines out there. We did not have any submarines because we had a fast ship, we could outrun the German U-boats! But thankfully we never did have problems with them going over or coming back to the States. They started to have radar and stuff in those days during the war which I am sure helped us out.

We finally landed in South Hampton England if I recall. We were in England for some time. While there, I had one pal who became a good buddy, but we got separated after a while. Not sure what happened to him. Then we went across the English Channel. Further east there were landing spots, there were just a couple of villages where we got our feet on the ground. We didn't see any of the towns. The German's had guys all over there (France). We had to cross France. It took us about over a month from England until we finally got to the War front in the middle of the country where the German army was fighting, it was already late in 1944.

I was a Jeep driver and I drove for the Communications officer. I had some freedom and flexibility so, I did a little hiking around. One time I was recruited because an officer needed a Jeep to get around to keep in touch with other outfits, to see what is going on. So, I drove him around which was a pretty important job as a jeep driver. (Shows us a picture.) Those are all my buddies from my company. In the company they had different outfits some of them had rifles some had machine guns. Well I didn't have anything because I had to drive. Lieutenant Cornet was a wonderful man from Bluefield West Virginia. And boy was he ever smart! I don't know how he did it, but he always seem to know exactly where the enemy was! I never knew where the hell the enemy was! I wasn't sure where I was! But, he seemed to know everything, which gave us a lot of confidence in his leadership.

After the war was over, he wrote me a couple letters. Unfortunately, you know after a while I started throwing everything out, I threw uniforms out, insignias, blue pins. I've done some crazy things in my life. Now see this writing, you ever seen more beautiful handwriting. Same amount of space here as here, it's all free hand. (Shows an example).

Well since not being on the front line like a foot soldier, sometimes I was pretty far back like from here down to the corner. Sometimes the front line of battle could be a mile away. At one point our outfit had captured a German bridge which they did not have time to blow up! We had the trucks and the troops go over the bridge. That was the first victory so to speak. We lost two of our men in Germany one afternoon when there was some heavy bombing and shelling going on by the Germans. The same group of us soldiers fighting were only a couple of blocks away from the enemy. After the firing stopped me and one of my buddies went over there to see if anybody got killed. Two of our boys were laying on the side of the road on their back dead. I went there and it seemed to me that my blood just left me and went out the end of my feet! I can't explain to you, the blood that was in me flowed down to my feet and left me. I didn't pass out, but I sure felt like it.

The first dead German soldier I saw, was while we were in a bunker. Because the Germans had bunkers and the French had bunkers too. The bunker is basically underground with an entrance facing the lower part so you could walk in and out. And up above they had one of the sections a little hole or opening so you could look out the thing. Well the first day we were there I went out in the morning to take a leak. And I damn nearly tripped over a dead German. He must have been a scout or something and somebody that had guarded during the day must have shot him. But we didn't hear a thing because we were dead tired and asleep. Inside this bunker you wouldn't hear a thing anyway because it was solid concrete several feet thick and there was no door on it! And I looked out and it was just barely getting light. The poor guy must have been there all night because it was cold and he had turned all green. Well, the medics came around that pick up dead soldiers, and wounded soldiers too and treat them.

My best friend here, Frank F., he was a medic. So, he had to go out wherever there were dead or wounded to pick them up and take them to base hospital or morgue somewhere. Or sometimes they gave them first aid right then and there you know to do whatever they can do for the person. Then they will take them to a small hospital which is further back behind the lines.

NEAR THE END OF THE WAR:

The United States didn't get to Berlin because for whatever reason we wanted to let the Russians to get there! The damn fools! We could have been there days before the Russians. And they let the Russian's get in instead! This country does some stupid things, like I do stupid things sometimes! Why they stopped say five or ten miles outside of Berlin I don't know. They knew where the Russians were, they knew where the Germans were, they even knew where Hitler was! In his bunker down under some place. And we could have gotten to Berlin first! Why they didn't do that I don't know. I don't know who made the decision that we're going to stop here and we're not going any further. Eisenhower or somebody way back in the States I guess, who knows. Politics, I guess.

As far as Hitler, they don't really know what happened because he died in his bunker. At Burgess Garden near Bavaria he had a special retreat in the mountains of Germany. It's a place that's away from the cities and towns. He also had a girlfriend, Ava Brown. I believe she got killed with him.

WAR AND FEAR OF DEATH:

I wasn't afraid of the war; I wasn't afraid of being killed. I never thought of being killed. I don't know why. I probably thought, well God is on my side, I just don't know, but I never got as much as a scratch on my finger, nothing! Because in the service in the army, if you drew blood you get the purple heart. They were giving out a thousand Purple Hearts a day! To Everybody that had a bloody nose or bloody head or a bloody something or bloody anything! I'm getting to make it sound a little ridiculous, but that's how you got the purple heart, that's what the purple heart was for, because you were wounded. They were much more worried, if a bullet went right through your stomach or your leg. If you got a little scratch or drew a little blood; There were probably a couple of million that were wounded but never got the purple heart! The purple heart was just a name. Oh, of course some got seriously hurt, and suffered for hours and even days, and then died. Some died right away, which if I was hit, I was hoping that I would just go quickly; who wants to suffer for all your life? Some people suffer all their life, whether you're sick or get shot or something. Lay in bed all day. Well I don't want to do that. Die fast and get it over with!

FOOD & MEALS:

(How did you all eat?)

Well a lot of time it was on the road because when you're hiking or there's an engagement going on you don't have time to eat. Well a couple of times, we got a piece of chocolate! It was about this square (a couple inches). It was so hard you could hardly bite it, but it was full of vitamins; so, that's how you got your vitamins! It was terrible! It could take you an hour to eat that, to try and chew it up. It was so hard, but it was chocolate, and it was full of chemicals, but it also had all kinds of nutritional value and everything I guess. Other times they gave us canned food. Small cans about so big. (like a standard can of vegetables) The had one meal in them, rice, vegetables, I think.

Well one time one of my buddies and I, we had a little campfire going. On the ground you threw the can in to warm it up. We were too busy talking and stuff, when all of a sudden, BANG! You know what happened, the can blew up! There was somebody's food all over everybody's clothes!

PRISONERS:
(What about taking prisoners?)

The only time I saw prisoners was when they had given up already. By then the war was nearly over. That is the only time I saw several Germans; But there was a time we had captured two Germans. Our officers interrogated them, and they asked questions from them; what outfit they're in. You were supposed to give just your outfit, nothing else. So anyway, we captured I believe two German pilots if I remember correctly. So, our commanding officer our CO, right there where we were staying in the camp, started asking all kinds of questions! We wanted information about what the Germans were doing out there; The strength of the soldiers and people; what kind of planes they had. Things of this sort, everything related to the war.

So, this interrogating went on for quite a while, it wasn't hours, but at least twenty, thirty, forty, minutes something like that and neither of them wanted to talk too much. They did speak English, but they would not admit it. So, they would hear what's being called out in English, but they would say no we don't understand. You know what my CO would do when they didn't want to talk? He would order one of them, "Go behind the building," he came back to the front of the building to ask more questions for the other German soldier. When all of a sudden, Bang!! You know what that was! This was to pretend that he'd just shot one of the Germans. So, if he shot one maybe this guy would talk. But it was just a pop gun. It was just to let the other guy know; hey I'm going to get you because your buddy was just shot. But no, it didn't work, he never did talk. He must have figured, well he's dead! I don't know what happened after that, but anyway that's what he did. And

I think they got the information they wanted, and they let him go or probably put him in a prison camp. Now that was the closest, we got to Germans, except once the war was over.

NEAR THE END OF THE WAR:

Something that did happen when the war was already winding down. You know when there is a war, civilians want to go someplace where they are not going to get killed! So, there are houses all over the country, there was one house right next to us where we were camping. A beautiful brick house, about half the size of this house; it was a beautiful brick house. It was me and a fellow on the second floor talking, and there were GI's down in the first floor too. Just wasting time there was nothing to do, the war was over all ready. So, me and my buddy are talking, just shootin' the breeze you know. This door between two rooms and I'm standing like this, talking to the other fellow sitting down over there across the room. So what happened, we hear a shot, a rifle shot. GI down on the first floor, I don't know how he did this, it was an accident. He shot his rifle an M1round came up through the floor, ripped part of this door down like this! The wood splattered all over me and I'm standing right there! This how close I was to getting killed! By accident of friendly fire no less! That was the close one!

GOD IN WAR:

God was with me then too as He is now. Just remember no matter what happens in life, God is with you; Remember that! God is with you whether you know it or not. Tell your parishioners Reverend. Yep, to this day you know I'm 99 and He is still giving me the strength. I still have a brain. It's not working the way I wish it was working, but it works. And I got a lovely family, a lovely daughter and three sons even though I am still able to live alone, and they are all still in heart.

HIS KIDS PHOTO:

I keep pictures of my children, and Mary my wife. I kiss these guys everyday They're my heart and soul; Suzanne, Arthur, Frank and Andrew.

AFTER THE WAR:

After the war, I got married to my dear wife Mary. We were married nearly 70 years! I had a sister and a brother in law that lived in Toronto, Canada with my mother-in-law where my wife Mary came from. Well my sister and brother-in-law first went to Montreal Canada, while I was still in Hungary at the time. This was in the far back as the late 20s' or early 30s' he came home one time he came back to Hungary from Canada, I remember he came home to visit. And this was before the war.

They had a cottage on the lake called Stony lake in Ontario, Canada. Ontario is huge! I believe it's bigger than all, the size of all of New England and New York state put together! A great big province. So anyway, every time we went up there in the summer for two weeks my wife and I we'd go to her mother's first in Toronto. And then we would go with them to their cottage for a week. My brother in law built that cottage. He had a job but every weekend after work Friday he'd rush up there Friday night! They packed food like everything they needed and went to the place to build the cottage. This cottage was right on the lake, built on a high hill. Stony lake is beautiful! You have to see it I can't fully explain it! When you're out there you can see nature, the birds, and go fishing! Just quiet; peace and quiet; except for the birds and all singing. We spent a week there; we had a room that was like a little kitchen, with a big front window, overlooking the lake. If you open the window you could jump right into the water! You were up high around 20 feet high because like I said it went down from the road like this, on a grade. But the cottage was on stilts. On top of that he put this cottage. But he had stuff in there too, he built a bathtub out of wood for his wife, my sister to take a bath in, down in the basement. And he had water there not drinking water. It was pretty good I don't think it would kill you if you drank the water; there's no pollution over there that I know of. But it would pump out about 20 or 30 feet into the water to bring water in the water pump; he had everything set up. He liked to smoke so he rolled his own cigarettes. You get the paper, with loose tobacco and he rolled his own. He'd go in the boat, he loved to just be in the boat and throw the fishing rod and he didn't care if he didn't catch any fish, he was happy to do that, while he's smoking his homemade cigarettes. He did come home with a fish or two sometimes. We put them into a container, a box with wires on it and about so high and maybe about a foot or so square (like a lobster pot) and he put the fish in them, (like an underwater cage) Right in front of the cottage submerged in the water.

All in all I have had a wonderful family and a blessed life for which I thank God. I am truly blessed!

PHOTOS:

Left to right from top: Mayor of Norwalk Harry Rilling, Andrew Mantlik, daughter Suzanne Brennan, Lucia Rilling, mayor's wife. Andrew & Mary on their wedding day St. Ladislaus Hungarian Roman Catholic Church, South Norwalk, Conn. Son Frank Mantlik, Andrew Mantlik, daughter Suzzane Brennan. Veterans Day Ceremony November 11, 2019 City Hall Norwalk, Connecticut. (Photos by Rev. J.P.C., Editor.)

Dr. Albert Shansky: Medical Corp in France

Interviewed 12ᵗʰ of March 2019

DATE ENLISTED & BRANCH OF SERVICE: June 1943 Engineers
BASIC TRAINING: Camp Claiborne, Louisiana
THEATER OF OPERATIONS: France and England

I was born in Sheepshead Bay and attended Boy's High School in Brooklyn. At age 16 I started to work part-time after school in a medical dispensary for $45 a month. When I became 18, I worked full time. Shortly after that, I was drafted at the age of 18 into the US Army. I went from New York by train to camp Claiborne, Louisiana and was put into the engineers. This was my basic training. One day I had some time off, so I walked around the camp, and I saw the camp hospital.

I went into the hospital and I told them that I'm an experienced hospital lab worker in all areas of blood chemistry's and histology's and so on. They said, 'Well our T.O. is all filled up; but there is another outfit down below that might be interested.' So, I walked over to this outfit and I told them my story. And the Major said I can have you transferred into our outfit, but we are leaving for overseas. So, it took a couple of months in the states and then I was taken on. And I transferred all my stuff, my weapons, and everything else all over to this new outfit. Then they declassified me or reclassified me from the engineers into the medics. And so, I was with the 127ᵗʰ General Medical Hospital.

We departed for Europe on the French ship SS Normandy, I don't know if you recall or even have heard of that boat. There were 10,000 US soldiers aboard the ship! It took nine days to get across the Atlantic Ocean. We landed in the port city of Liverpool, England, of course later famous for The Beatles! Then we traveled by train from Liverpool to our site in what was called Taunton, Somerset, England. That is where we setup the hospital. An interesting side light of the story is that fact of being in England one whole year before D-Day.

Thirty-five years later in 1979 I went back to take a look at the place where the hospital was originally set up. It was set up on the grounds where there was a big mansion; and all the officers had rooms in the mansion. Meanwhile they had built these Quonset Huts, the larger one for the surgery and the smaller ones for the soldiers to sleep in. It was a very productive time. Because at that time the Americans had already entered the North Africa Campaign. The English and wounded American soldiers were coming back to England, and we were taking care of all these wounded soldiers.

JUNE 6, 1944: D-DAY!

My experience with the war at that time was the Germans bombing us! There was lots of bombing going on. After about a year training and preparing in this area, one day the whole outfit dismantled the hospital and put all of our stuff together and we went to Southampton. And we sat there, for the longest period of time. When one day the planes started coming back! You had never seen so many American airplanes, and British airplanes too. They were coming back, and we found out because Eisenhower was making the announcement that D-Day had started. We were all sitting outside watching these planes coming back and we knew it was D-Day of course. On D-Day+6 (June 12, 1944) we were put out onto a boat in Southampton, called the Star of India. We sat out on that boat for three and a half or four days. Finally, they put us out into the middle of the English Channel and we got off the boat, by ratlines coming down the side of the boat, into ducks (duck boats) which were called landing craft. That's how our whole outfit, came that way onto Utah beach. We gathered at a small town called Carentan, a French town. We stayed there for about another week. The Germans had been bombing while we were landing. There were paratroopers from the 101st that had gone down before us in parachutes which were made of White silky nylon. After landing, many of the parachutes were picked up by the local people because they wanted the parachutes material to make clothing and dresses and other things out of them. The look of that area where they landed, there were parachutes all over the place! The paratroopers just unzipped themselves from the equipment and kept right on going! After about a week passed, General Patton had come up on the beach while we were still there. We were assigned to General Patton's outfit. So, like a bee out of hell, we ran off these small beaches and followed Patton into France in this region called Brittany. We wound up in a town called Nancy, France. That is where we finally set up the hospital.

It was the most awful kind of thing! So many dead soldiers, and other soldiers coming back severally wounded, and all of us had to pitch in. I became a Litter bearer. I wore this yoke around my neck and slid the wounded onto the litter and brought them all back to the beach so they could transport them back to England into hospitals that were ready to receive them. In the meantime, we had set up our hospital in Nancy. What we did was we took over a French hospital and we would build it in Kassern which is a French army post. We were there for a while and then they needed some people to go further toward the front lines of fighting and so we got to the city of Trier on the German border. By this time winter had come. The Germans had started to return artillery fire, with those 88s' which are unbelievable! Bombs were coming over left and right and the snow kept coming down. And if you ever saw cold weather it was the coldest thing! It got so bad even some of our cooks, and any other available people all went into the Battle of the Bulge at that point. It was December 1944. The last gasp of the German army.

GENERAL PATTON and FRANCE:

People like me who were more experienced were left behind, and I'm very thankful that I never went into that battle. The fact is that they needed people like us to take care of the wounded. Finally, there was this breakthrough in weather and airplanes were able to fly over; American airplanes came over and bombed the Germans and stopped their advance, I should say their advance against us. We stopped them, at what was Bastogne (Belgium). When General Patton rolled through, our troops just kept moving forward you know; and really pushed the Germans out of France! The American troops followed General Patton into Germany, and we went back to Nancy, France. And that is basically… the whole story. That was actually where the war ended for us in Nancy, France. My discharge, says European, African, Middle Eastern service medal. Good conduct medal, and the Victory medal. I got three medals. More important on my discharge it says where I was located near where the city Trier was. Then I went back to Northern France.

France was a genuinely nice country and I happened to like living there because I learned to speak the language a little bit. I met a lot of nice people, and I made a lot of good friends. My closest buddy whose name is Harry Ault was a Hungarian. We had a first sergeant in our group who was also Hungarian whose name was Sivos, if I'm pronouncing it right S I V O S! They used to talk to each other in Hungarian.

(What was your most memorable experience?)

BLOOD CHEMISTRY & A SOLDIERS CANCER:

I hate to say it because it is difficult for me to tell you. That what I found was bad for the person I found, was good for me. I worked in the laboratory doing what is known as blood chemistries. You take blood from a person and then you do a blood count of white blood cells, red blood cells. These blood counts come in on a routine basis; everybody gets it. The soldiers who come into the hospital all get this. And it came to my desk and I found one guy who had lymphatic leukemia. Normally we have thousands of determinations going on, and you don't expect to have anything unusual happen. And here this poor guy comes in to give a little bit of his blood for routine testing purposes. Suddenly you find out he's got cancer of the blood. So, I went into to Colonel Curb the pathologist leader of our laboratory. Colonel Curb was a bit of a chicken colonel. The funniest thing is when I first met him in camp Claiborne, Louisiana, he was a major, and eventually he went up to Colonel. Anyhow I brought in the blood specimen and showed him the results. I then went back and got some more blood from the kid, and redid all the tests, as it had to be done. I went back and reported to Colonel Curb who said, "Well this poor kid's got cancer." And we're going to do what we can to cure him of that. In addition, he was shot a couple of times, not fatally, but enough to lose significant blood. That was a memorable experience, something that I didn't enjoy finding out, but knowing that I was able to locate this thing as a 19-year-old technician! But to be responsible for letting the powers that be know that this kid is not going to make it unless he gets medical help.

FEAR & THE BOMBING OF ENGLAND:

Oh, the bombings were terrible in England. We were in the city called Taunton and as I said, we had set up this hospital on the grounds outside of town where a large mansion was located. The mansion was located and had all these Quonset huts. That is one of the most amazing things about Americans, which I found generally everywhere. They are builders and they know how to build and build fast! They put up these prefabricated Quonset huts right away. Everything was brought in; beds and mattresses all that kind of stuff.

So, I went back 35 years later I wanted to see what it looked like. I could not find the place! 35 years since the end of the war, that whole area was all built up with little houses. Veterans coming back and British veterans coming back. Finally, I got a hold of an old contact, and I said, could you take me over there. There was no way I could recognize the road that used to go there, it was all redone and rebuilt. I finally got out there and I said where is the mansion? They told me, 'Oh they took that thing down, and they built houses out there.' So, it was a very unusual thing to happen after 35 years. It was not as big as Levitt town, back in the states on Long Island, but it was a small village going up.

There were other reasonably important things, but to me they sound so silly. Well I mean, I made friends with a lot of British people and, I went to their homes and so on. I never really faced death; I spent my time in the army helping somebody else. Helping somebody who's infirmed or wounded or on death's doorstep. I even had a stint in the morgue. I used to look at these cadavers these, dead bodies, and I would say to myself, 'you know I hope there's a better place for this person.' I try to do what I can to prevent this from happening to someone else. That's why I feel doubly different about the young boy whose cancer I discovered. I'm hopeful and I think he probably was in some way cured by the American medical system. It was a fabulous medical system, that they had in the United States Army.

My experience with the actual war itself was the bombing of England. And there were times when we were hit with bombs, it was not as bad as it was at the actual front where the airplanes would come over and they would bomb the airfields. We were next to an airfield also and there was a lot of air activity going over it. D-Day + 6 it was different because there you had to do whatever you could to keep up with the soldiers at the front so to speak. But basically, I did no fighting. All of my war experience had to do with taking care of soldiers medically. I saw a lot of cases of PTSD, which it wasn't called that then. It was called "war fever" or shell shock in the First World War. I was happy to finally get out. I did it (my duty), but I wasn't really in anyway a harmful situation. But I did my duty.

AFTER THE WAR: BACK HOME

I got out went back to college and I got my bachelor's and master's at Brooklyn college. And my PhD., at Illinois Institute of technology. I met my wife Pearl when I got out of the army. We lived next door to each other in Sheepshead Bay. She was still going to college, and I just started when I got back; so, we went to school together. Then we started dating and shortly after that we got married in 1948. And after 73 years of marriage, here we are still together!

(What's the secret?)

The secret is… I don't know what the secret is. You might be interested we went on our honeymoon on a hitch-hiking trip. (Like in the movie "*It Happened One Night,*" Frank Capra?)

Well, yeah like that, similar. We started out on the subway; we took the subway all the way up to the George Washington bridge. Then we walked across the George Washington bridge! And then I thumbed rides and it took us two days would you believe it? We got enough rides and I think we went to Marcy, New York or someplace in upstate New York and we stayed overnight.

I kept thumbing and we came to Montreal! I said to Pearl my wife let's go to Outremont which is a suburb of Montreal; maybe we can see Uncle Himey. So, we went. This is the God's honest truth; We went to Outremont on Van Horn Street. While we are walking down the street, I said to Pearl; 'Who is that? Isn't that Uncle Himey?' There he was standing outside the Synagogue, with a bunch of people! He was so thrilled and happy to see us, and we had a nice visit. After a time, we hitch-hiked back through Boston; we came down through New Hampshire, Vermont, New York, and home. And we had a wonderful time. We slept in hotels and motels.

Later we had our four children and seven grandchildren and three great grandchildren.

(EDITOR NOTES: I went to first & second grade with Richard their son at Fitch elementary school!)

LIFE & MEANING:

(What is the essence of life?)

I don't know how to answer that; I really don't know how to answer that. It changes, it changes over the years... I'm 94 years old and it changed over the 94 years, and now I think of life as being something that's still continuous for me. I spend time daily writing my books. I'm on my 15th book. I gave up teaching about three years ago. I still lecture every once in a while, when people want me to. But it's really, about staying active, I'm just an active person; and the meaning of life is that life goes on, it's as simple as that.

Left to right from top: Albert Shansky in uniform; Dr. Albert Shanksky in His study in Norwalk Connecticut; more Albert Shansky in uniform; Albert and Pearl in their lovely home after 73 years of marriage.

Uncle Frank Anastasia: Philippines

(EDITOR NOTE: I interviewed my uncle Frank back in 1999)

The Anastasia's had a large Italian family of 11 kids. The six boys, Sam, Frank, Edward, Patrick, Anthony, John were known as 'the Saugatuck boys' from Westport; They played softball. And Five of the boys all except the youngest one, were also in WWII. John became the deputy chief of Police in Westport, Connecticut. The five girls were Mary, Josephine, Anna, Eleanor, and Florence.

When WWII broke out Frank like so many others joined the service. He ended up in the Pacific theater in New Guinea and then eventually the Philippines. At some point they made him a cook because I guess he was good at it! He also took up boxing in the Philippines. The Filipinos love boxing and so they took a liking to him, which is not hard to imagine, because everybody loved uncle Frank! I have been known to joke around at times saying my uncle was Manny Pacquiao's godfather! Well, one day during the war they said we want you to meet our champ and box him. So, initially excited, he got into a jeep or truck with this gang and started out, and suddenly thought better of it, not knowing where they would take him or how big this guy might be! So he came up with some excuse to return to base.

Another time he told me there was apparently a JAP sniper hiding in the brush or trees near their base of operations. And the Sergeant or officer sent Uncle Frank to go find him as they would hide out in the coconut trees! Understandably he was scared so he walked down a path a bit of ways and heard something moving in the grass and I think he said he shot a cow!

My uncle often showed us a photo he kept from the war of a young Filipino boy age 12 or 13 that use to help him I guess in the mess hall and with the cooking and I think he kind of took him under his wing. Many were orphans. I think he regretted he did not get him to come to the states after the war for perhaps a better life. My uncle Frank had a generous heart, and would give you the shirt off of his back.

My aunt Dee told me the story when their first son Frankly Jr was born during the war in 1944 I believe. Uncle Frank had won money in a crap game and got leave to come home! So, he made his way by train all the way back to Connecticut to see her in the hospital and the baby. She was so happy, but she stayed strong and did not want to cry in front of him.

He told me towards the end of the war, especially after VE-day and the surrender of Germany, the US troops in the Pacific theater were preparing for the invasion of Japan. It was estimated it would cost the lives of over 1 million soldiers and civilians! So of course, our troops were elated when the war ended after we dropped the atomic bombs on Hiroshima and Nagasaki, forcing the surrender of Japan.

(EDITOR'S NOTE: We often attempt to interpret history through our modern lenses, which is not always the proper focus shall we say. Many of the veterans I have interviewed over the years, if not All, said the same thing; the Atomic bomb as horrible as it was, saved many countless lives by ending the war. Of course, it ushered in a new era of the Cold War and the threat of Nuclear War giving to man for the first time in history the unthinkable ability of annihilation of the human race. But perhaps more frightening is to consider what if the Nazis or the Japanese had gotten the bomb first!)

My cousin Franky Jr. also went into the Army around 1962-65 stationed in San Antonio, Texas, and Germany. After the war they had another son William (My Cousin Billy who became a Marine) and a daughter Rosemarie. Billy served stateside during the civil unrest of Vietnam protests in 1968-70. His son Christopher, Frank's grandson became the third generation Anastasia family veteran, as a major in the Army in 1990's at Fort Bragg and also served overseas in Kuwait.

He and my aunt Dee lived upstairs from grandma and grandpa on 18 Elm street. He told me one time his son Billy was only 2 or 3 years old and fell down the stairs. Uncle Frank threw himself down the stairs and managed to catch him by the foot on the last step before he went through the glass doors! They both came out of it OK!

Uncle Frank would always play with us kids or watch cartoons. He was a like a kid at heart. He took my twin brother and I fishing for the first time at Broad River. And they took us to Playland in Rye New York. In our big back yard, he taught us how to build a fort out of sticks and weeds and grass, probably something he did often like a lean-to in the South Pacific during the war. He always made pizza on Christmas Eve for us. He worked for Borden's Milk and would bring us orange-aid and milk shakes.'

Uncle Frank was well known for the expression you 'Dirty Dog.' It's on his tombstone along with a song by Bob Marley which we sang at his funeral, *"Don't worry be happy!"*

That was Uncle Frank. We still miss him, and always will!

Letter to his sister Mary while Somewhere in the Pacific Islands during WWII.
Uncle Frank & Aunt Dee circa 1980 at their cabin in the Poconos Mountains, NY.
Frank Anastasia Sr. 1942 Army Uniform: Often people would say my uncle Frank looked like the actor, Charles Boyer.

Helen Czsel Fumo & Peter Fumo

(Story told by Patti Benson, her second born daughter)

Helen B. Czel born on Dec 20, 1921, was the daughter of the late Josepf Czel and Suzanna Czel. Helen lived in Norwalk, CT most of her life until she moved in with her daughter in Redding, CT in 1997 where she lived till 2005, when they moved to Austin, Texas.

Helen B. Czel enlisted in the U.S. WAC (Womens Army Corp, with nearly 150,000 other American women) on August 5, 1943 at New Haven, CT. Helen received her basic training at Fort Devans, MA. She was sent to Mitchell Field New York, and after serving there she was then sent to Wilmington, NC. And after more training Helen was sent overseas to the Pacific sailing out of Stockton, CA., on an overcrowded troop ship. For a short time she was stationed in the Philippines, then permanently sent to New Guinea. Helen worked in the mess hall and wherever needed. She was honorably discharged from the military service of the United States of America on Nov. 5th, 1945.

Helen and her late husband Peter were great lovers of baseball and avid Mets fans. Later in life Peter was an umpire for over 15 years for the local Babe Ruth Youth baseball league of Fairfield County Connecticut where they lived.

She and Peter had known each other before the war, having grown up in South Norwalk with its large Hungarian/Italian community. Peter joined the Army on May 5, 1942. He was a cook in the US Army and landed on Anzio beach, Italy. It was no picnic!

In July of 2013 she was selected by People magazine in conjunction with Major League Baseball to attend the 84th All Star game in New York City, where she represented the New York Mets.

Helen volunteered at St. Mary's Church in Norwalk, CT., as a Sunday school teacher when her two daughters were growing up. Helen was also a member of the Catholic Women's Club bowling team of Norwalk, and was a member of the local VFW.

Later in life she moved to Austin, Texas with her daughter Patti and son-in-law Kenny Benson. Her daughter Linda back home in

Connecticut would send her wool remnants, and Helen would knit hats, by the dozens! She did this for more than six years, (till she could no longer knit due to arthritis) and the family would donate the hats to the local Merritt Street homeless shelter. She loved her family and her grandchildren and great grandchildren and had a wonder life of 96 years! She was buried with Military honors at Arlington National Cemetery.

Left to right from top: Helen Czel Fumo, circa 1945; Helen Czel Fumo at a NY Mets AllStar Game Shea Stadium, Queens New York, July 2013; Helen Czel Fumo circa 1942; Husband Peter Angelo Fumo, circa 1944

Uncle Anthony "Bucky" Tavella:
3rd Army with General Patton in Europe

Fought with the 3rd Armor division under General George S. Patton.

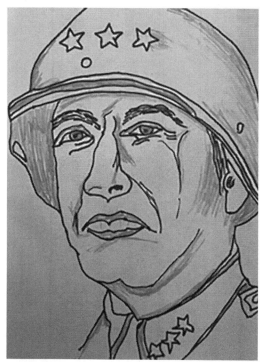

Sketch of General George S. Patton, by Beatrice Robertson, Bucky's niece and goddaughter,
(used with permission)

(EDITOR'S NOTE: Some recollections of stories my uncle Bucky told to me.)

Bucky was one of ten children, from a large Italian/American family. His father like many Italian immigrants was employed in the Hat Factories of Connecticut. He died tragically before there were strict Osha laws and regulations overseeing factory workplace . He had gotten a brand-new pair of shoes and proudly wore them to the factory. But sadly, as I recall my uncle recounting the story, he slipped at work due to the new leather shoes, and fell into a vat of acid used in processing, and sadly died from his injuries. He is buried near

Bucky's in-laws, my grandparents at St John's cemetery in Norwalk.

My uncle, like many Italians was shorter in stature around 5'2". But he had a big heart! And I think as often happened even in the military he was picked on somewhat. The Sergeant one time told him, "Hey Tavella, go clean out that barn!" Apparently, some German soldiers were hiding there. And He did it!

Another story I believe was from him, is coming upon a farm house in the French countryside that had just been hit by a large artillery shell which blew out the entire side wall of the house but otherwise left the structure standing and intact. As they approached the exposed room was the kitchen and seated around the table was the entire family seated in normal positions seemingly without injuries, but who were all deceased. Apparently, the shock wave from the blast literally blew the breath of life right out of them! Very sad.

My uncle loved to drink loved milk. It was only served on the captain's table for breakfast. He didn't care. He went over and drank it! One time they were in a village, and the civilians there were hungry. He had an orange in his hand. And this young German gal came up to him and took it and ate it! Of course, he didn't really mind, and let her enjoy it.

My uncle Bucky fought with the Third Army under General George Patton and received a letter of commendation for it. (I have misplaced the copy.) He and my father took my took brothers and I fishing off the rocks at the end of Neptune Ave after the bridge fell down around 1965. Being a rookie fisherman and brothers and I only had a light string drop line and no lead weights. He fixed us up with some heavy cord line and tied some old pieces of asphalt onto it from the broken-up roadbed, and I caught my first little flounder! I took it home and cleaned it and cooked it on the Hibachi grill.

He bought me and my two brothers canons when we were little and would love to play army. I'm not aware of my uncle staying in touch much with many combat buddies. He seemed to want to forget the war. He worked as a carpenter and contractor, and was good friends with fellow veteran Dr. Alan Shanksky. (See his story in this edition). My uncle built little Cape Cod homes including the one he my aunt Frances lived in. She was my mother's only sister. Same mother but different father. They never had children of their own, so my mother's five of us became like we were theirs too! My sister still lives in the house he built with his own hands after the war.

Left to right from top: Also called Tony Tavella, he made corporal; Uncle Bucky at Anti-Air-craft gun range; Bucky Tavella at boot Camp; Uncle Bucky and his Sargent with the helmet, out on maneuvers in a 'duce and a half' ton truck. Uncle Bucky, Aunt Frances (my mothers half sister) and an unknown Tall Dude! Bucky with his Thompson machine gun.

Robert Leitton Sr: Europe Liberation of Camp

As told by Rev. Robert Leitton, Jr.

WAR AND LIFE MEMORIES & EXPERIENCES:

My dad was in World War II, third armor division, with (General George Patton) One of his last acts was to be riding in the lead vehicle that went through the gates of Norheiman, (This is his recorded name of the location) concentration camp. My father told me his lead vehicle literally tore down the gates as they went through! He said when they got inside the compound itself and came to a stop a man came up and climbed on top of his vehicle and said "You're American?" And my father answered him and said "Yes!" This gentleman, now a freed prisoner said, "I studied at your great university in New Haven, Connecticut." (Meaning Yale) And my dad started a conversation with him. My dad told me he then reached into his army backpack and gave the man, who was obviously malnourished, a can of condensed milk. A simple act of kindness he said he should have never done. Because the man drank it and died at his feet!

When people have been starved for so long you literally cannot just start to eat. Because it is a shock to the body, and it was just too rich for him. Till' the day my dad passed away he cried every time he remembered that story. What my father didn't realize at the time is that his mother, lost family members there at Norheiman; my grandmother's family.

My father was a Lithuanian Jew. We did not know that until after we started to do some research. I have a family picture with my grandmother. So, when we went to Israel, we visited the big Holocaust museum that they have there in Jerusalem. We met people that were actually part of our family heritage from there and began to talk to them and started a dialogue. My grandmother lost all of her brothers, her mother and her father in the Holocaust. Her one brother, they were able to get him out before they were all picked up, and he is the one that kept the family line going.

My dad took a brief case and a gun, and the shoulder strap from a German prison guard that was there at the camp. The last time we went to Israel we took it with us and donated it to the museum there in Jerusalem. I'll never forget, on his dying bed he cried remembering that powerfully sad story.

Part 2: ARMY AIR CORPS (Air Force)

William Hudak

DATE: April 12,1943 Untied States Army Air Corps (Force)
BASIC: Fort Deven's Mass. & Shepperd field, Texas
THEATER OF OPERATIONS: China, Burma, India "CBI" stationed in India

C-46 William Hudak standing in right

As told by his son Robert Hudak:

Dad was a sergeant with United States Army Air Force. His occupation was an aircraft painter with the 26th Repair squadron in the China-Burma-India CBI theater of operations. He did general painting work on the interior and exterior of all types of aircraft and equipment. He also did fabric and dope repair (a type of glue) on flight surfaces.

He also worked on the Curtis C-46 commando (see Photo) which

was a twin-engine transportation plane that was the largest twin engine plane in World War II. This plane was painted olive drab green
on the top surface and robin's egg blue on the lower bottom surface.
(This enabled it to blend in the sky when viewed from below.

He oversaw a five-man crew engaged in this work. He was also
stationed at a B-29 Superfortress bomber base, located in India, and
flew over the Himalayan mountains.

Doug Clarkson

Amanda's grandfather is a WWII vet and served as a B-24 nose gunner in the 15th Air Force European Theatre. Staff Sergeant Clarkson completed 50 missions and while his plane always managed to make it back to an Allied airbase, on several occasions the B-24 had to be scrapped due to significant battle damage.

For the past 10 years, Doug and Mary Clarkson have been regular attendees at Sherman's Special Person's Day — 3 of their grandchildren have attended Sherman school.

Douglas A. Clarkson, The Home Front circa 1944

Alexander Grey, Edie, Florence, Douglas Alexander Clarkson

Douglas A. Clarkson (rear row ?), B-24 nose gunner, 50 missions.
15th Airforce, 461st Bomb group, 764th Bomb Squadron, Cheryonla Italy.
(Metal fragment - German shrapnel sliced off the heal of Doug's boot, in flight)

Douglas A. Clarkson, B-24 nose gunner, 50 missions completed.
15th Airforce, 461st Bomb group, 764th Bomb Squadron, Cheryonla Italy

All of us have always been very proud of Dad's military service and over the years we heard stories of his missions (as well as his antics).

Dad graduated from Greenwich High School in June 1943, 6 months early so he could enlist in the Army Air Corps, his preference over the regular army. He was sworn in on graduation day.

Basic training was in Greenville, NC then Dad was off to Lorado, Texas for gunnery school. Next was Chatham Field, GA for a crew assignment and more training.

In July 1944 Dad sailed to Naples Italy via North Africa. When he reached Naples his crew was broken up and he was assigned to a crew that had lost the nose, waste and tail gunners while they were flying as substitutes with a different crew. (Crew members were allowed to fly as substitutes on additional missions to complete their tours sooner). Dad stayed with this crew his entire time in Europe. The pilot, Stanley S. Skalanski, was a "training" pilot, a designation reserved for only the best pilots.

Dad was a Staff Sergeant assigned to the 15th Air Force 461st Bomb Group, 764th Squadron based in Cherynola, Italy. He flew primarily in a B-24 as the nose gunner completing 50 missions.

The primary crew — pictured in the attached photo are:
First row (L-R)

❖ Pilot: Stanley Skalanski, Squadron Leader, from Chicago

❖ (The ship was named Iggy after his girlfriend, sometimes a jokester would use tape and change it to "Piggy". Dad admitted he was the instigator and often the one who did the taping — this admission was to me, but not to the pilot.)

❖ Bombardier: Sherman S. Goodfriend, from Chicago. He flew additional missions because he liked "the power" — he also became lead bombardier placing Dad's plane in the lead of their squadron.

(Dad said he threatened to kill Sherman on a mission because he would not open the nose door hatch and let Dad out when they were ordered to lighten the ship, claimed it would be too cold.)

❖ Navigator: Meserschmidt

❖ Co-pilot: Gross from Michigan. He ultimately took over as the pilot.

Rear row (L-R)

❖ Mechanic, Ben Barefield from Ozark Alabama, in civilian life was a linesman.

❖ Waist gunner, Waldo Mckilson from Hazel Run Minnesota (he described it as a bend in the road with a telephone pole).

❖ Radioman, Tope, was airsick all the time.

❖ ? is Dad—a bit of humor.

❖ The tail gunner, Bill Bower, Pottsville, PA was a baker (his father and brothers were coal miners, but he could not stand that work). He was part of Dad's original Georgia crew assignment and was credited with shooting down ½ a plane).

❖ Ball gunner, Bob Irwin had one leg shorter than the other. He covered this up so he could serve in the military. He was married with a child.

Highlights of Dad's time in Europe.

One of the substitute bombardiers was so scared that he would build a nest of flack jackets and stay there for the mission. Dad would be the one that pressed the bomb release button since he could clearly see when the lead plane dropped their bomb load.

On one of his first missions the glass bubble in front of Dad was shot away. He flew back with just the bulletproof glass panel in front of him—cold, yes it was. When he was asked why he stayed up front for the return trip his response was—since glass and bullets don't mix well doesn't this happen all the time. The answer was no.

Bombs were activated shortly after takeoff. When the target was socked-in, the bombs had to be jettisoned prior to landing by dumping them in the Mediterranean or over land. Dad recalls flying low over Italian fishing boats and releasing the bombs nearby. No one got hurt but the fishermen would not have enjoyed the experience. On another occasion the bombardier saw what he called a good target, a white church in a German town and asked if he should release on that since they had to jettison the bombs—Dad said the entire crew told him no.

Another favorite was to drop coke bottles out of the plane at high altitude over enemy territory. As the bottle fell to the ground it made a whistling noise similar to a bomb. These bottles were sure to have scared more than a few folks on the ground.

As a nose gunner dad hit an enemy fighter once. He watched as the bullets bounced off the underside. No damage, no one hurt, but hopefully his shooting helped keep enemy fighters away from their ship.

On one mission shrapnel hit a plane flying in the "box" with Dad's plane. This caused the bombs to release prematurely and fall on the plane flying directly below—both planes exploded and took out several additional planes nearby. Dad's plane was blown sideways by the blast and was critically damaged. They completed the mission but when they made it back to base the plane was junked.

While Dad never had to bail out there were several close calls such as the one noted above. On 2-3 missions Dad's plane had to land in Northern Italy since the plane was unable to make the trip back to Cheryonla. Dad does recall on one such mission that his crew used the money from their "escape kit" to pay for food and supplies from the British after they landed. After several days they were picked up and ferried back to base.

Dad did have one exceptionally close call. He had a piece of shrapnel cut the heal of his boot off. He was not hurt but a new pair of boots was in order. On several other missions the plane was badly shot up including holes in the wing where German anti-aircraft rounds had passed through. These rounds from German 88s did not explode on contact because they were set to detonate at a higher altitude.

WOW!—Dad's thought when he saw German fighter jets for the first time. They would shoot through the Allied bomber formations from high altitude at incredible speed but did not carry enough fuel for multiple passes.

While in the Army Air Force Dad enjoyed a good smoke particularly at 20,000 feet with pure oxygen in use. It was fun to inhale the oxygen and then blow out through a lit cigarette—creating a blowtorch.

On his last mission the crew threw a party that included throwing the chaff out of the plane while traveling home over northern Italy. The problem—the chafe messed up allied radar—the outcome was a directive from the 15th air-force that no more chafe was to be thrown out over friendly territory.

On the ground

Life was not that bad. The food was all right (especially since dad actually liked Spam) except to this day he still laughs because he cannot figure out how they made instant mashed potatoes that were "lumpy."

Dad was not concerned about being killed since he was 17-18 and it was always the other guy, not him.

One morning Dad was awakened by a friend that had been on a plane shot down several weeks prior. He managed to allude capture and ride the German rails back to the allied lines. This was particularly ironic since these same rail lines were the targets of many of the 15th Air Force bomber missions.

"Playing with fire" — one of the guys on the base was a pyromaniac and liked setting off signal flares. On one occasion he lit red "emergency flares" for fun and caused a general's plane to abort a landing. The following day a directive was sent to all bases ordering that no flares be used unless there was a legitimate emergency.

Trip back home

Dad shipped out of Naples. The ship was filled with 1/3 air force, 1/3 Canadian, 1/3 German prisoners.

While waiting to ship out Dad's group would play the regular Army guys at Craps. When the German bombers flew over and all the lights were shut off Dad's unit would always win. (There were more Army Air Force guys in these games so who would argue that they did not win.)

On the trip home Dad, along with everyone else threw most of their stuff overboard. He and everyone else just did not want to be bothered with it — they could get more when they arrived back home.

The shipped docked in NYC on Easter Sunday 1945. Dad found out later Aunt Edie was in NYC the same day but neither knew how to get in connect with the other.

Back in the U.S.

Upon returning to the states Dad was taught to be a gunnery instructor in Lorato Texas. He then taught new recruits gunnery in B-29s, which had remote turrets. On one occasion while training he recalls shooting off the rounds in the 50-caliber machine gun by just holding down the trigger, emptying the gun fast and thus allowing them to return to base sooner. This overheated the gun and when it was placed back in the rack it "popped" off several rounds that shot holes in the tail of the plane — a B-17.

After arriving back in the U.S. for a short time Dad volunteered to go to the Pacific theatre. He did not like the regular army formalities (spit & polish) vs. the interaction of officers and enlisted men in the war zone. The war ended before he was taken up on his offer. He was honorably discharged in Montgomery Alabama in October 1945. He used a $400 bonus from the state of Connecticut to buy his parents their first color TV! In fact, his parents were the gardener and maid on the Jerley estate, and Mr. Jerley, who did not own a TV, would come down to the Gardener's house to watch the fights with Dad's father.

Anonymous: B-17 Nordan Bomb Site

WWII ARMY AIRCORP: B-17 NORDEN BOMB SITE BOMBARDIER

F___ was my barber. His father I believe had started the business when he immigrated from Italy many years prior, and F___had taken it over. One day getting my haircut he told me this story.

He was trained as a bombardier on the Norden bombsite, (which happened to be manufactured in my hometown area of Norwalk and Stamford Connecticut).

But the story took place on a bombing run over Europe in WWII. The B-17s would depart from their bases in England, across the English Channel, and head to Germany to unload their deadly cargo. His squadron had 9 planes with 9-10 men in each B-17, and there would be three squadrons in his Group, for a total of 27 planes. The three would fly staggered vertically with F___group on top and the other two flying below.

Literally hundreds of planes participated in these bombing daytime high altitude bombing runs. On this day run, as they are heading to Germany, there were three other Squadrons in a Group of B-17s returning from their bombing run. The Groups were to operate on varying horizontal or vertical coordinates for obvious reasons of airspace safety and risk of accidental running into friendly allied planes.

On this particular run someone terribly failed in their proper coordination of position. The two squadrons below F___ ran directly into two returning squadrons of fellow B-17s! F___ said, 'We were helpless, and all we could do was watch the 9 planes from each of the four squadrons collide into each other!' All 36 plans were lost and with them the crews of over 350 men! It is not known but perhaps some men were able to parachute to safety. F___s squadron completed their mission and returned to base.

They day he was sharing this story as I was getting my haircut at his little barber shop, I ran to the car to get my tape recorder. As soon as I returned, he clammed up, and did not want to speak of it anymore. I began to learn in those days when I started this project of collecting War Stories, how difficult it must have been to live with the horrors of war. And then to return to a society that was largely ignorant of wars real cost. And people who mostly just expected the soldiers to carry on, and resume living, in the words of Marie, the wife of bombardier pilot Fred in the movie, "*The Best Years of Our Lives*," 'just as if nothing ever happened.'

The Tuskegee Airmen

The Tuskegee Airmen were the first of their kind, comprised in WWII of an All Black (of African-American and Caribbean- born military pilots, including pilots from Haiti, Trinidad, and Dominican Republic; See Wikipedia) United States Army Air Corp forces included, the 332nd Fighter Group and the 477th Bombardment Group. They are named for the base from which they trained, in Macon county, Alabama. They also took the name *Red Tails* for which a film was also produced.

Their accomplishments are virtually unparalleled in the annals of WWII, as they flew fighter escort for the B-17 fortress bombing runs over Europe with no losses! In spite of their status as United States military men, they still experienced discrimination in and out of the army. But the skills they displayed in combat and the distinction with which they served paved the way, for the eventual, and long overdue, desegregation of the armed forces by then President, General Dwight D. Eisenhower. Korean would be the first war that American servicemen served in a fully integrated manner.

EDITOR'S NOTE: We were not able to get permission to copy the story of retired Col. Charles E. McGee, or Calvin J. Spann, both Tuskegee airman from WWII. But we wanted to at the very least, acknowledge their exceptional heroic war service to our country. Also recommended for further historical information on the role of African Americans in the military; The Civil War film *'Glory'* and study of *The Buffalo Infantry Soldiers* of WWI.

Part 3: NAVY: Coast Guard & Merchant Marines

Uncle Tony Nardella in his own words: USS Minneapolis, Pacific Theater

DATE ENLISTED: Joined the Service in 1943, on April 13. Was discharged in 1946.
BRANCH OF SERVICE: U.S. NAVY BASIC TRAINING: Camp Pendleton, CA.
THEATER OF OPERATIONS: Pacific, U.S.S. Minneapolis, light cruiser.

I was born in Scranton PA, on July 24, 1925. (Age 75 at the time of the interview). My dad died 1928 when I was three years old. I lived with my Grandma, and my mother re-married, Antonio Esposito. In our day we grew up on hard times. (Scranton was a coal mining town and it was the Depression) I shined shoes and delivered papers. (I saw my uncle Tony's pink shoeshine box, he still had it!)

At age 16 I joined the Conservation Construction Corp and went to Brandy Virginia, along with a buddy Joe Pinnead Tuves. 1940 we hitch-hiked home October 31st. In 1942 I worked for one year with Bobby Pinna in Philadelphia to learn welding. Once I shined a college kid's shoes and he gave me a dollar! So, I went to shoot pool! We had lottery and gambling then called the numbers. We also would shoot craps, stuff like that at the DeAquino club, which was a neighborhood hangout.

North Scranton Bulls Head, on Doal Street is where I met Aunt Connie. (My Aunt, his wife!) Her father (My paternal grandfather) was from Nicastro, Catanzaro, state of Calabria in southern Italy. He was very strict and did not allow his daughters to even hang around boys. One night I was talking to her on her porch and she saw a man walking down the street. She said, 'It's my father!' So I ran from there through cold dust back yards and allies and got filthy. It turned out later, it was not him!

MOST MEMORABLE EXPERIENCES:

When the war started people felt patriotism and bought war bonds to support the effort for $25! In one of our first battles the ship had taken three torpedoes at Guadalcanal; Blew off 80 feet of bow, gone! We paid four dollars to the natives, who used coconut palm trees to reinforce the ship. We proceeded to Pearl Harbor, then on to California. It was June 1943. All this time on ship I was never seasick. We arrived back at Pearl Harbor September 1943. On October 5, 1943 was our next engagement battle at Wake Island.

We rescued two pilots and returned back to Pearl (Harbor). For the next 30 months we traveled all over the South Pacific. We fought in 12 to 13 battle engagements; The only other ship with more was the USS Enterprise Aircraft Carrier.

My job was damage control, R – Division, stationed three decks below. On one occasion we were refueling at sea, with an English Tanker manned by Hindu sailors, when a Japanese Kamikaze (suicide plane) hit the Tanker ship! There was no explosion, but it listed. We picked up the survivors. We also had a 500-pound bomb was dropped and hit the water right next to our ship. It put 140 plus holes in the ship. R – Division had to plug holes with welding. No lights at dusk, so we plugged the holes with mattresses and bulk heads.

After this the Captain gave us liberty in Padre Ho beach in China, which was inhabited by White Russians. 15 of us went on land, for a big gig, outran a guard and stayed overnight on the beach. In a school 500 yards away, the Japs were firing at us.

I met a nice Italian person that day on the beach. Next day, at a little diner breakfast cost 45 cents for Steak and Eggs. After breakfast I got drunk on Vodka. My buddy tried to sober me up! He said I kept calling for Connie; We finally made it back to the ship.

It would be 11 months before we got back to Pearl. I went ashore twice, once in the Philippines Island Mindanao. We drank two cans of warm beer, and I met a girl. Her name was Consetta, whose grandmother was praying to the Virgin Mary. A big black US soldier came along and threw me out of the house! I guess for my own good! Then finally back to Pearl for R & R (Rest & Relaxation); and once again across the Pacific to the Philippines.

Once there we met up with the Japanese fleet, in the Surbahars (Luzon?) Straights. We sank a battleship with our eight-inch guns! Saipan, Tinian, another new duel battle and on to Gilbert Islands. The bombarding of Okinawa, and Iwo Jima are two major engagements we missed and did not participate in.

We were one day behind the USS Indianapolis. The Indianapolis was a sister ship to the Minneapolis and had a terrible fate after delivering the first atomic bomb to be dropped on Hiroshima, Japan. We were supposed to have the Atomic assignment, of delivering the bomb. They delivered it for the B-29 bomber the Enola Gay, but we ended up picking up survivors of USS Indianapolis, after it was torpedoed by a Japanese submarine. (Out of 900+ men only 300 survived after several days in the shark infested waters where many succumbed to shark attacks and the elements.)

I read Captain Charles B. McVay, was court-martialed and years later committed suicide at his home in Litchfield, Conn. in 1968 (see Wikipedia) They subpoenaed a Japanese Admiral who defended McVay and whose testimony exonerated him and said, he did his job well. The Japanese and everyone vouched for the Captain! The B-29 flew out was the 'Enola Gay'—which bombed Hiroshima. And the next B-29 was 'Box Car'—which hit Nagasaki. The Japanese surrendered September 2, 1945 with Admiral Nimitz, General MacArthur and others aboard the Flagship the USS Missouri. After the war our ship the U.S.S. Minneapolis was docked at Philadelphia, then later scrapped.

AFTER THE WAR: I came to Connecticut on June 1, 1946. I stayed at Connie Cardamone's then, September 2, 1946 we got married. We had three children, my wife was a real home body: cooking, baking, and cleaning. After I retired we had a close-knit family and six grandchildren.

ADVICE FOR TODAYS FAMILIES:

Discipline kids: say no sometimes. Recommendations: live within your means, stay away from debt, use common sense, you don't have to be a genius. There is more bankruptcy today. We never paid interest for credit cards. Also know where your kids are and who they hang out with. Don't be afraid to go into their room. Do things as a family; make it a plan to go on vacation.

Clockwise from top: Tony & Connie courting and having fun! Connie & Me engagement

EDITOR'S NOTE: When my third son Micah was born in 1998 my uncle Tony was a volunteer at the Norwalk Hospital. We talked about my small investments at the time, and I was asking his advice about investing in the Stock Market. He pointed down to the baby in the bassinet and said,

'There is your stock!' I never forgot that!

For additional reading: See the book "The Minnie" about the USS Minneapolis.

Uncle Carl Pierce: USS Wisconsin

PHOTO below: the EDITOR'S son Luke's personal model:
IOWA Class battleships also included the New Jersey, Missouri (Model below), and USS Wisconsin BB 64,

As an original crew on a newly commissioned ship, my uncle Carl told me when I was a boy, they were entitled to a plank on the deck of the ship! Battle wagon BB-64 as she was referred to was launched December 7, 1943 at the Philadelphia Naval Shipyard on the second anniversary of Pearl Harbor. Her nick name was 'Wisky' (see Wikipedia). With nine 16-inch guns she really packed a punch! He always said they should have signed the Japanese surrender on the Wisconsin, but because President Truman at the time was from Missouri, he picked the Big Mo, as she was called!

After the war he settled in Norwalk and was married to Mary Cardamone, my father's oldest sister. He worked as a house painter, with my uncle Frank and my father for a while. He and my aunt Mary raised two beautiful daughters, my older cousins Carol & Mariann.

He worked for himself as a house painter for many years and I can still remember him painting the peak of our house on Lockwood lane when I was a kid. He was up there hanging off of that ladder like he was on the side of a ship!

He took me to my first college football game to see the UCONN Huskies around 1966. It was cold and rainy day, as we watched the game and my cousin Carol who was a cheerleader for the team, and he bought me a hot dog. On our way driving home, we had a flat tire and he taught me how to change a tire!

His life was not easy, he had his struggles, and he lost his dear wife my aunt Mary when she only 54. But everybody loved him and his winsome smile and sparkling blue eyes. St. Patrick's Day I think was one of his favorite holidays and we always remember him fondly that time of year!

There were six planned but only four IOWA class battleships built prior to and during WWII, the last of their kind.

*Left to right from top: Example of a 'Plank Owners Certificate' from a friend Jim Stenger:
Please forgive the Mermaids lack of modesty! Uncle Carl's future wife Mary Cardamone
with her younger brother Dominick, my father. Proud Grandpa Cardamone and Aunt Mary
his oldest daughter, on her wedding day at 18 Elm Street, Norwalk; Carl Pierce & Mary
Cardamone Wedding day Norwalk Methodist Church; Uncle Carl's future brother-in-law
Frank Anastasia (with his future sister-in-law Mary Cardamone), Carl's future wife! Carl's
daughters my cousins Carol & Mariann with Santa and below my Mom Annie hugs Santa!
Uncle Carl on right, my Pop Dominick next to him, Billy Abbott & unknown friend
on 18 Elm Street.*

Mike Salvatore: C.B.'s Construction Battalion in the South Pacific

(As told by daughter & grand-daughter Jeanne Frances Salvatore. Interviewed May 2020)

Michael Salvatore, Father: WWII Navy CB, Construction Battalion

Jeanne is born in Norwalk in January 1934 to Vivian Van Wagner (who lived to age 104!) and Michael Salvatore. After Pearl Harbor Mike joined the service for four years, starting in Hawaii as a CB engineer cleaning up and rebuilding the damaged Pearl Harbor.

Near the end of the war he was then sent on what was known as the Philippine Assignment with the 142 U.S. Naval Construction Battalion. They were located on the island of Calicoan in the Philippines to supplement the construction forces engaged in preparing the Leyte area for use by future post war naval activities. This area is well known for the great Naval battle of Leyte Gulf, considered the largest naval battle of WWII fought in October 23-26, 1944. The US and allies alone fought with over 300 ships against the Japanese Imperial Navy. It was also the first time Japanese aircraft carried out organized *kamikaze* (suicide) attacks against America forces. (SEE Wikipedia)

THE PHOTOS: the following are uncopyrighted photos from Michael Salvatore's Philippine Assignment, 142 U.S. Naval Construction Battalion, yearbook, used with daughter's permission.

William Van Wagner, Grand Father, WWI Navy:

He was stationed I believe out of the Brooklyn Navy yard. He went to sea in the North Atlantic, aboard a ship unknown. While at sea he was wounded in battle. The injury developed into a staff infection (this was before penicillin was available) and resulted in the loss of his leg. He was hospitalized in California veterans hospital for re-hap and to be fitted with a prosthesis. He eventually returned to Norwalk and worked for many years at Nivea cosmetic factory on Water street.

Left to right from top: Water Pipe line Construction; Water tank being built; The Camp; Civilian Girl grinding corn. Freighters at dock, and artillery gun. The aerial view of camp.

William Van Wagner

Julius Kish: Navy USS Lexington

As told by wife Anna D'Amato Kish

THEATER OF OPERATIONS: U.S.S. Lexington, an aircraft carrier, and other ships spent four years in the Pacific Navy WWII.

My husband would describe when our planes got shot up, and when the pilots returned, often there would be a fiery crash landing! And the sailors had to hose it down! They used foam. Unfortunately, lots of guys were often killed on the flight deck. On more than one occasion Jules almost died! God was looking out for him! My husband use to say, 'the Japs could never find our ship!'

(EDITOR'S NOTE: The first USS Lexington (CV-2) was nicked named 'Lady Lex' with only one other ship in her class USS Saratoga. The Lexington was lost during the Battle of Coral Sea in May 1942 when she was heavily damaged by Japanese forces, and had to be scuttled, the first carrier sunk in WWII. Her wreck was discovered on March 5, 2018, See Wikipedia.) There was a second ship USS Lexington (CV-16) Essex-class carriers which began service in 1943 a total of 14 ships, the key strength of the US Navy! (see Wikipedia).

(EDITOR ASIDE NOTE: After the War, my father built houses with Ted Cromwell, a master carpenter from Norwalk who also served on the USS Saratoga in WWII. Uncle Ted as we referred to him, years later gave me a baseball he had gotten in a pickup game while in Honolulu. It was a foul ball that was hit by the great baseball player Ted Williams who was in the service! While visiting friends near Boston in Summer 2004, I gave the ball along with a baseball card of Ted Williams to my buddy Bernie who had two sons that were Red Sox fans. Being Yankee fans ourselves, my sons and I also said a little prayer to 'Break the Curse' of the Bambino. No brag but Boston won the World Series that year!)

USS LEXINGTON STORIES:

Honolulu: Once at dock he was in a bar and this guy Frank Bashey who was from Norwalk, and who had come into Honolulu (on a US destroyer) walked into the bar! Jules said it was good to see an old familiar face from back home.

Clockwise from top right: Julius was 17 years old in this photo when he enlisted in the Navy. This is a family neighborhood photo welcoming Tony back home after the war. A few years later when he worked at Perkin-Elmer doing Optical engineering, got his first car.

WWII ARMY:

My brother-in-law Steve Kish was in the Army First infantry division in Europe one of the first guys to enlist in Norwalk from Lexington Ave. He had a lot of stories including landing in Normandy on D-day. He fought in many of the major battles of Europe and on one occasion while in a fox hole his sergeant was killed beside him and he himself was wounded, shot in the leg. He walked with a limp the rest of his life. He attended the 50th anniversary of D-Day in Normandy in 1994.

My oldest brother Tony, they called him 'Winky' was also in the Army as a paratrooper and landed on D-day into German occupied France. He was wounded, shot in the stomach landing with his parachute. The Germans took him prisoner. He came home at the end of the war and lived to around the age of 87.

This is a family neighborhood photo welcoming Tony back home after the war. That's Pop in the middle with the white shirt and tie, (He was big shot with the Democrats in town) Ma to his right. He also was an Italian barber on Woodward Ave, she was Slovak and they had 13 kids together. My mother cooked that day for everybody in the picture! Tony is in front of them and that is me second from his right. I'm born in 1929 so I guess I must be around 15-16 years old.

COLD WAR ERA: Army

(EDITOR'S NOTE: Even in time of the Cold War accidents and tragedies can happen, reminding us of the risk all our troops take while away from home and overseas serving our country.)

Photo of my nephew was Joe Pantalone. He was a very handsome fellow, who married a nice Italian girl from New Canaan; She was very beautiful and looked just like a princess on their wedding day! He played basketball while attending Trinity college.

In the ARMY he was stationed in Morocco North Africa. He was killed there in a car accident in 1974.

He and six fellow Army buddies were driving to play basketball. It was foggy, and their car was hit by a bus, and they all perished in a fiery crash, and had to be identified by their dog tags. Back in the states they had a closed casket funeral. I still think of him and my husband, and brother often and miss them everyday.

T.D. Navy D-day: USS Laffey

Recorded May 2000

THEATER OF OPERATIONS: US Navy: USS Laffey, Atlantic D-Day

EDITOR NOTE: We conducted a recorded interview over 20 years ago and this veteran who has since passed away in 2006. At the time of publishing we were not able to reach his family for confirmation to use his name, but we feel strongly that his War Story is important to remember.

A World War II U.S. Navy veteran, T.D. was a Gunner's Mate Third Class having served aboard the USS Laffey. He was a recipient of the European African Middle Eastern 1 Bronze star, Philippine Liberation Ribbon 2 stars, Asiatic Pacific Theater Ribbon 4 Bronze stars, Purple Heart, Victory Ribbon, and American Theatre.

T.D. in his own words.

During the D-Day invasion we were supporting the landing by shelling the beaches to soften up the German resistance for our troops. We being a destroyer had a shallow draft and therefore could get in close to the shore and fire our Five-inch guns. At one point a German artillery shell hit our ship in the front bow but did not explode!

It wrecked our Sonar and electronic detection. We had to send a crew into the damaged bow area to evaluate and disarm it, which they were able to do. When we opened the shell there was a note from some military factory forced laborers from Czechoslovakia I believe, who said they had intentionally sabotaged the projectile so it would not explode! God and destiny were on our side.

(EDITOR'S NOTE: In every interview I have conducted with veterans there is always an emotional highpoint I call it. It is probably the reason many are often hesitant to talk about their experiences. The emotions of recounting these stories become over whelming and the person often begins to cry. Ii is my hope and pray that this is in some way a cathartic experience for the individual, as they feel someone else finally understands the trauma they lived out in the war.)

COAST GUARD:
Jim Hastings USS Manhasett & Son Jimmy Navy USS Kitty Hawk

Jim Hastings Coast Guard WWII North Atlantic

(EDITOR'S NOTE: This story is told by his wife Irene Hastings. She is my oldest church member who at age 98 [February 2020] still lives alone and drives herself to church!)

I met Jim when I was around age 16 or 17 at a feast they use to hold on Strawberry hill in Norwalk. I would go with my girlfriends, which was the site I believe of the old Devine family farm, and it is now Nathan Hale Middle school. We were married in 1942. He spent two years on the East Coast on a ship **USS Manhasset** out of Boston, looking for submarines in the North Atlantic.

(EDITOR'S NOTE: The ship was a commercial cargo ship which during WWII the U.S. Navy would lease. It was equipped with guns and depth charges and used as a weather patrol craft and convoy escort. She had a total of 150 officers and enlisted men and experienced action in the dangerous North Atlantic, guarding against German U-boats, but survived the war. Manhasset an American Indian name which was from an inlet hamlet in Long Island Sound, New York. See Wikipedia).

My son Jimmy was also in the Naval reserves stationed in Guam during the Vietnam era in the 1966-68.

Jimmy Hastings now tells his story: I spent 18 months on what we called 'The Rock' the island of Guam. (EDITOR NOTE: it is U.S. territory won after the Spanish American war of 1898; see Wikipedia). Temperature averaged 90 degrees year-round. I was a mine man 2nd class. (Dealing with land mines). From Guam I went to the USS Kitty Hawk aircraft carrier. They let me out three months early. It was going to Nam. (Vietnam) I don't regret going into the service. I think some type of military service should be mandatory for all young people in our country.

Jimmy enlisted age 21 Naval Reserves; Canon outside administration building on the naval base on Guam; Irene with nephew Dave Zavory a Vietnam veteran.

PEACE CORPS/AMERI-CORPS

EDITOR NOTE: As most veterans have told me, 'The service helps you grow up and teaches you about the real world.' This editor thinks we should have some type of national Peace Corps or America

Corps or call it whatever, but a mandatory service for all young people getting out of high school. They put in a year of boot camp and training, and then a year of service, not necessary military. There can be several tracts of study such as nursing, trade school, law enforcement, and the kids are sent around the country or overseas as good will ambassadors. They get to see the world a bit and grow up and get a taste of what they might want to do with their lives. In return they get college tuition paid for at any State school.

MERCHANT MARINES: J.J.

My last recorded interview with J.J. was in February 2020 while he was hospitalized and then in re-hab. Unfortunately, J.J. passed away shortly afterwards, before publication was finished. His daughter gave us permission to share his experiences, anonymously.

DATE ENLISTED & BRANCH OF SERVICE: 1943-45 Merchant Marines:

THEATER OF OPERATIONS: Ships in Atlantic & Pacific theater

WAR TIME EXPERIENCES

One of our first voyages out we were leaving port out of Newport News, Virginia when the engine blew! Since we were off the east coast out to sea in the Atlantic, the captain gave us a choice of going back to Newport News, Virginia, or Miami! Needless to say, we had a great month in Miami! They guys all had lots of fun!

On our next Atlantic trip, we took a convoy of 19 Liberty cargo ships from New York heading to Belgium. Only Seven ships made it! German U-boats sunk them, about one every night! That was despite us having destroyer escorts. Each night we would lose about one ship, but we were Not permitted to stop! We hoped our Navy destroyers would pick up any survivors. We also were not armed.

The Liberty ships were mostly old boats from WWI and were not built very sturdy. They kind of slapped them together in about a week. One hit with a torpedo and they just fell part! Because we were losing so many they came up with the idea and started retro fitting them with a steel belt that wrapped around the whole ship! This helped hold it together a little better in the event of a torpedo strike.

For our Pacific trips we took the Panama Canal. We visited Papua New Guinea, Australia, New Zealand, and the Philippines, ferrying supplies for the war effort. Everything from food to ammunition. On the return trip we would head into San Francisco.

I loved my time at sea, and I think I was a better man for it.

EDITOR'S NOTE: The Merchant Marines were finally given Veteran status and recognition on January 20, 1988. These sailors had a higher death rate in WWII than the Army or Navy and lost over 700 ships sunk. (see article LA Times January 30, 1988 by Eric Lightblau).

CIVILIAN: Sonar Engineer: Blaire Benson

EDITOR'S NOTE: Although a civilian, we have included Mr. Benson's profile here because of the strategic nature of his work in sonar which was a tremendous contribution toward the Navy's military success.

(As told and drawn by son Kenny Benson. Also see The New York Times Sept 8, 1990)

My dad was exempt as he was an engineer at GE working on developing sonar in Top Security. My mom was working there too at the time.

Investigation of the use of echo-ranging equipment or an "active" homing torpedo system was initiated under the auspices of NDRC in 1941 at the G.E. Co. Research Laboratory, Schenectady, N.Y. Active homing differs from passive homing in that, with active homing, the torpedo steers on the basis of the signal returned by the target through reflection of the torpedo's own transmitted signal. In mid-

1942, G.E. began development of the first active homing torpedo, Torpedo Mk 32, which was physically similar to Mk 24. They worked in Bridgeport, CT and never said much about it except that it was TOP SECRET at that time.

(EDITOR'S NOTE)

The beautiful Jewess actress, Hedy Lamar, at the time of WWII, was also involved in developing a similar torpedo and actually contributed significantly to the war effort because of her gifted and innovated scientific mind. Not just a pretty face on screen, as a Jewess she had a strong desire to help free her people from Nazi tyranny. (Reference, Turner Classic Movies).

"MOVING THE WAR" is also an excellent video, highly recommended for other war stories produced by a college friend of mine Marco Ciavolino. It is some of the moving stories of the crew members of the more than 1300 WWII LST fleet ships, including that of his father Michael Ciavolino who passed away in August 2019 at the age of 95. They literally moved the men and material that won the war, including the atomic bomb.

As they said,

"You did a lot of growing up! As a 18-19 year old kid, you learned so much and you did things you never thought you could do!"

"It brings out the best of the potential in you!"

"You realized the United States is the greatest country in the world!"

"A lot of people died doing a job that had to be done, and they should not be forgotten."

We hope to share some of these stories in future editions of *"War Stories & Remembrance."* (see USLST.org). (youtu.be)

PART 4: MARINES

Robert Lanehart: Iwo Jima

(EDITOR'S NOTE: The following are recollections of interviewing my neighbor back around circa 1995.)

Bob & Doris lived next door to me during my first pastorate in Georgetown CT. (1992-2002). They were both wonderful people who our four boys have fond memories of. We use to have chickens in our barn, and the running joke was, 'Why did the chicken cross the street?' The Answer: ' To get to Mr. Lanhart's yard!'

One day there was road work going on and they were digging up the street with big tractors and machines. I'll never forget Bob came out and said, 'It sounds like a War going on out here!'

Bob inspired this project in many ways and shared many of these stories with me.

He was born and raised in Westport. When Bob enlisted in the Marines at age 17, he visited Mrs. Dunnigan's home to see Doris his sweetheart, before shipping out. Being a tall fellow, put a hydrangea flower into the chandelier in the front parlor. Well the story goes, Mrs. Dunnigan left the flower there until he returned home.

After boot camp at Parris Island Bob went on to Camp Lejeune. From there shipped out to the Pacific. There were many tedious hours of boredom on board ship. Bob liked to read. This boredom however would be followed by intense battles!

Bob served his country on the military campaigns for the islands of Saipan, Tinian, and Iwo Jima. On one occasion I believe, they had all got drunk on this Pineapple Fruit Hooch, as he called it like home-made Moon shine! And then they were in the landing crafts, waiting to hit the beach, the boats driving in circles, and riding the waves, waiting for their time to land, and smelling the diesel fuel smoke! That's enough to trigger my vertigo and you know what happens next! Lots of men had to vomit over the sides or into their helmets!

Once they landed it was not easy to move around on the volcanic sand of Iwo especially with the Japs shooting down onto the beaches. There was lots of death, bodies and the smell all around you. He said the smell is something you never forget. One of the first tasks as engineers was to clear an area and move some heavy mines. Bob being a fairly big guy was carrying two of these mines. His two other buddies were only carrying one each and so were walking faster ahead of him. A Japanese mortar shell came down in front and I believe killed both of his buddies. He was saved only by walking slower.

Another time on Iwo he carried a flame thrower on his back. They had something like a 75% mortality rate because they made such a good target! Well Bob fell into a cater, or big hole onto his back and could not get up, like a stuck turtle! And at that point he realized he did not have his 45-side arm on him either! He was a sitting duck, but, as he would say, 'The Man upstairs was watching over him!'

After the war ended Bob served two more years in China and played football on a military team of veteran's who did a good will tour throughout Asia. Doris Dunnigan had to wait a little longer, but he finally arrived home, and they were married September 23, 1950. Bob made up for lost time and had 6 wonderful children they raised at the old homestead there on Smith & Church Street in Georgetown. He said many nights we would wake up Doris, yelling with the bad dreams of battles that stay with you the rest of your life.

Bob became a lineman for C.L. & P. (Connecticut Light & Power) and worked for over 37 years. After retirement he stayed involved with the Marine Corp league, Lions Club, and Sacred Heart Church. Every morning Bob would faithfully and proudly raise the stars and stripes on his flagpole in the back yard. And every evening retire the colors. His kids had given him a T-Shirt for one of his birthdays which read:

'NOT AS LEAN, & NOT AS MEAN,
BUT STILL A MARINE!"

He always maintained that handsome, crisp, neat, Marine decorum. And when I was moving away, he asked me, when his time came, to be sure and say a few words over him. In later years when we would visit, he and Doris, after they had to move to an assisted living, he would remind me of this request, which of course I gladly assured him, I certainly would.

Well unfortunately, I missed his funeral. So, let this serve that purpose now. It was my honor and privilege to be the next-door neighbor for 10 years of Bob and Doris Lanehart. And I tried to raise my four boys there to honor and respect his service, sacrifice, and character of dignity that he displayed for all to see and admire. He truly exemplified 'The Greatest Generation!' I am afraid we may never see that caliber of character again in our country. They were a generation refined by the struggles of The Great Depression and The War. But we must never forget the fact that they saved the world for liberty and for that reason we shall forever be in their debt.

SEMPER FI! Rest in Peace Good Marine!

Rev. J.P.C.

Bob & Doris Lanehart's old homestead, Smith Street West Redding, Connecticut (Georgetown). Bob Lanehart's Flag pole from Church street, Wilton, Connecticut. They lived on the border!

Bob & Doris Lanehart circa 2017 at the Brookdale Home in Wilton, CT

John Kosar: Guadalcanal, Peleliu, Okinawa

He was born in 1921 and at time of interview on March 12, 2019 he was 98. I visited him outdoors in April 2020 in the midst of the COVID-19 pandemic to celebrate his 99th birthday here in Norwalk Connecticut.

(As told in his own words)

I was born in New York City and moved to Norwalk as a child, growing up on Ely Avenue and lived in South Norwalk much of my life. They called it Whistle-Ville back in the day. I remember the De-Vito's store on Ely avenue. There was Aitoro's appliance: they had a place there years ago. Now they are on Westport Ave in a real nice store. I guess the son took over the business from the father. So, I knew a lot of them, and lot of my friends down there were mainly Italian and Hungarians in the neighborhood like my wife who was Italian.

She was what you call... Napolitano! Her people were from the area of Naples. I met my wife home on leave from overseas during the war. She and I got to know one another, and I married her when I got back. Her name was Celeste Gilberte. Her father's name was Tony Gilbertie. He had the Norwalk Green Houses at the time on Isaac Street. And he had a brother who had the Westport Green Houses. I guess they still have the place down there, in Westport.

(EDITOR'S Note: I have seen the 100 year old lemon tree, started by the grandfather in the greenhouse at Westport!)

THE WAR:

I was in the first Marine Division. My neighbors the Lametta brothers were also Marines in WWII. I knew all the brothers very well. They lived down here on Newtown avenue; I think one of them still has a house down there. . I was in my early 20s' when I started in the National Guard here at the Old Armory which was on West Ave. down at the bottom of hospital hill here in Norwalk. I got out from there and went up to Springfield, Massachusetts to sign up with the Marine Corps, for four years in the First Marine Division! We were the first division instated by the Marine Corps. Before that the Marines they were all regiments. Then we became the first Division, and the by the time the war ended, and I got out of service, there were I believe five divisions!

Of course, the war started for us after the Japanese attack on Pearl Harbor. We shipped out and went down through the Panama Canal, on a ship which was a luxury liner. Once through the Canal and into the Pacific we headed to Wellington, New Zealand. It took us one month to get to there and we were stationed there.

GUADALCANAL:

The day before we made our first beach landing, they told us that we were going to make our landing and it was going to be the real thing. And everybody had to take care of themselves. If somebody got wounded, they said don't worry about him; keep fighting! And like I say, that is how it happened! When I look back at it, I realize it's crazy you know. When we made the landing, we caught the Japanese by surprise in the Solomon Islands, an area called Guadalcanal. That was the first offensive we ran against them. After fighting we used to go to Australia for a period of time, to recuperate and them we went back in and we hit them again. We were kind of surprised too, that we beat them!

I was never scared, when I think about it now, I'm still here 90 some odd years old and I never worried about anything like that. I sprained my ankle one day running and jumping in a fox hole! You had to be quick because the Japanese used to come over from their base and they would bomb us every day! They had a place up on the hill, where they lived, and we finally took it over. They called it the Pagota. And the Japanese would use that as a sort of a target mark since they knew where we were! And they would come over every day in the v-formation the planes and they would bomb us! At that time, our planes would be based on the Aircraft Carriers, since it was at the beginning of the war, and we had not yet established or built air bases. They would takeoff from the Carrier and we would watch them up there fighting the Japanese!

The Japanese would never break formation. They would keep in that V-formation because, as we found out later, the lead plane knew where to land in the Islands. Because they lived on the island and were familiar with them, so they had to know where the hell to go, and navigation was not as sophisticated like it is today. Since you knew the pilot in the front knew just where to go, the others would follow him. And you know because they could easily land on the wrong island, since it's all water all around; you don't want to die! Many pilots did die whether fighting in the Pacific or Europe.

I could say when I look back at it, I'm still here! I never did anything but sprain my ankle that's about it. I never got hurt; I didn't know what the hell the word scared was.

We would have the landing crafts that go over the side of the boat, you'd get in a landing craft you drop into the boat. And then you go into what they called "rendezvous areas," where they give you the orders to head for the beach; At the signal you all go!

We didn't have that many things to carry back then. Today it's a different story they got a lot of bags. We didn't have that kind of junk to carry we just carried ourselves and our rifles and ammunition. Our guns were made in Springfield, Massachusetts so they called them the Springfield rifle. They were not automatic they were one shot a piece you know.

(Did you have any prisoners?)

Not that I know of. When we would capture a prisoner, we would often feel sorry for them. I could remember sitting there once, and they came in and surrendered or whatever they do when they surrender. You're out there in the jungles and they would take all the clothes their wearing and they would just wear a little bebe shorts. To show you that they were unarmed and didn't have any ammunition. And they would come in and sit down and I could remember one time we're sitting there on the stone wall and they came, and they all just sat down! We always had cigarettes back then, I don't know how the hell come we always had cigarettes; but I offered him a cigarette. And they get up and bow to you and said "oh eeh." (Japanese)

I felt sorry for them. Because I figured they didn't know what the hell they were doing. Even as our enemies they were just following their leader's orders. Tojo (Emperor of Japan) and Adolf Hitler, who committed suicide, both of them were leaders of the two Axis enemy countries and they didn't want to be captured by the United States!

(What did you think about the war from a political point of view; did you feel patriotic?)

When I look back at it now, I see a distinction with the war in Europe, which we had two of them; World War I and World War II. And like I was saying Italy was always our ally in the WWI and after a time changed to be our ally in WWII.

But it seems to me that the war was different in Asia. By that I mean the Japanese and the nation of Japan was trying to conquer all of the Pacific Ocean region, even as far as Australia! But many of the Australian people, having British ancestry, were already over fighting in Europe, as part of the British empire! So, we had to protect the Australians and the New Zealanders, because many of their troops were already fighting in Europe.

So, because of this they were glad to see us! We would go over there and like the time in New Zealand before we made the first landing... then I was in Australia and we made a second landing and after that we were in New Guinea and a couple of other islands there.

(When you made landings did you have to go in small boats the duck boats?)

You got in the landing craft; the big boat has the landing craft on them. And you let the boat down and you got down on a rope ladder from the boat down into the landing craft. And you would go around in a circle and when you got the word, you would all head for the beach. Yeah, but the part you usually get a big kick out of is, when I look at it now is how it wasn't always so easy to make it to the beach! But what would happen is that we had our ships out there would be bombarding the beach with big guns, they would sit out there to bomb.

We had some of our big Aircraft Carriers and Battleships, and cruisers out there and those battleships like I say would fire with their big weapons, broadside you know and clear the beach for us. The Japanese would run into the hills and hid in caves and the like which would give us a chance to land. And once we landed, we got some of the foxholes the Japanese had built! I felt sorry for a lot of them,

I do even today when I think about it. Looking back, I see it was so senseless. And now here we are years later, by that I mean we're good friends with Japan now if you think about it, and even Germany as well.

(What was it like to hear those Battleships firing?)

Yeah, we had some terrific battles against our Battleships I'd say. We had one of them got hit broadside by Japanese. The Japanese planes used to drop their bombs and go low down to the water and hit the side of the boat to try and put a big hole in the boat so now you were taking on water. Some of those ships would be listing on an angle because they would be taking in so much water you know. The Japanese would fly in close and low along the water, where the anti-aircraft couldn't get them. They would try to do is, because they wouldn't just want to go in to bomb the ship, but they wanted to dive into the boat and kill themselves! Kamikaze pilots' and they're committing suicide, which I guess they thought that was a great honor because they were so desperate as a country. I can't understand that, I don't know, like I say a lot of it made no sense at all. When I look back at it now if I was to run a war, I would change some of the dumb things that took place; in fact like most all of it! Including even being there to begin with! Period! War is kind of senseless if you think about it, putting so much resources into destroying things rather than working together to get along and build things.

Well like I said I had brothers. I had a brother in the Air Force who was stationed in the United States in Florida. And I had another brother who fought the Germans in Germany. And he made it through safe and came home and all that and was fine. Then I had other people I knew in the service who went to war, in Korea and Vietnam. And one fellow took it pretty badly and he came back to the United States and was up here in a nursing home. One day he left the nursing home and he went along I-95 thruway on the overpass and jumped in front all the vehicles and the cars going down the road and was killed! Very sad. He just snapped and couldn't take it, and he went out of his mind.

(EDITOR'S NOTE: PTSD, Post Traumatic Stress Disorder, is a

very real problem with returning military personal who have experienced the trauma of war, including today. Awareness more recently of that fact that suicide continues to be a very real risk and we must do more about caring for our returning veterans.)

END OF THE WAR FOR ME: (VE day and VJ day)

I remember the end of the war. I figured you know it was about time that we were going to beat the Japanese and we were going to beat the Germans. I didn't ever think the opposite that we would lose the war. In 1944 before the war was winding down, we were going to hit an island of Peleliu off coast of the Philippines. But my outfit was getting out of there since my time was up. My Captain wanted to see me and wanted to know if I wanted to sign over for more. And I said, "No thank you," I want to go home. And so, I started to make my way home. I reached California by boat. I hear my outfit hit Peleliu off the Philippines, they took a hell of a beating. But they beat the Japanese anyway but still with a lot of loss. I had guys who lost their eyesight, lost their arm, their legs. And I come home all in one piece, I didn't even have a headache. The one thing I had was a sprained ankle. So I came home before the war was actually over. Oh, I knew people who were still in it. I knew, Charlie F. was in our outfit he was a nice Italian boy. He stayed in the Marines. But when I got to the West Coast like I said, the Division hit Peleliu. He got the Congressional Medal of Honor; he came home to receive the Award and he joined up again with the Second Marine Division they formed. And he went back overseas and fought in Peleliu where he was killed. And that was the end. I don't remember where he was from. We were all New Englander Marines. We're all from up around here: Connecticut, New York, New Jersey.

YOUR VIEW OF GOD & FAITH IN THE MIDST OF WAR:

You know when I think about it back then, I didn't worry about God or all that. You get in your fox hole and say, "Oh please God!" Well, you didn't do that, you just did what you had to do to stay alive. Today it's different I have more faith. Today I go to bed every night now and I say my prayer and thanks to God, Jesus, Mary and Joseph! For keeping me on earth in good shape and keeping my families in wonderful shape also and happy, and all my wonderful friends. My friend Tina here, wonderful person too, a very nice Italian woman. Yeah, I've had quite a few Italians friends and I was married to an Italian. I say my prayers every night, I talked to God every night I say to Him I hope they give me time to still be here on terra ferma good ol' earth you know? Because I got a wonderful daughter and a wonderful son and a wonderful grandson, daughter-in-law and all and I want to enjoy my time with them!

HOW YOU WERE CHANGED BY YOUR EXPERIENCE?

(Did you ever have any nightmares about the war like many veterans do or PTSD?)

No, never bothered me. I had a lot of dreams; I dream a lot but what I dream about is a lot of crazy things happening in the light; but it never really took place with me. In different stages of my life doing things you know when I was younger and all in my dreams, those things never happened in real life. And I think about how come I'm dreaming about something that never took place. Unbelievable, the way our brain is still functioning.

I don't think PTSD was much of a problem. I think you had it in Korea and Vietnam and places like that, but far as WWII I don't think I've ever heard cases where people had stress and what not. They did what they had to do and that was it. No, I never worried about it, I never worried about getting killed or wounded or anything. You did it and that was it, I don't know what I think about it today and here I am sitting around 90 some odd years old.

YOUR VIEW ON THIS PRESENT GENERATION & OUR COUNTRY'S DIRECTION:

I always think, even to this day and age I believe the United States of America is the strongest nation in the world. We have bases in the Pacific many people may not even know about. We have a base that's out there in the Pacific they call Guam. It's a nuclear base and they could fire missiles from that base in the Pacific Ocean and hit any target in the world. In other words, if anyone started any trouble, maybe even the Russians as far away as they are, we could hit Russia. And

Russia is a big country but it's a lot of wasted space! Almost goes all the way to our West Coast here. My theory today of the world is nobody's going to do anything in any country. No other country wants to get into wars so let's forget that. No other country's going to start any more conflict the way I look at it. Because one thing is that we are a powerful nation and I could tell you we got bases all over with our allies all over the world. And they're all going to stick with the U.S.A!

John & Christina a caregiver; Driveway party for John's 99ᵗʰ B-DAY!
John age 99 July 2020 outside his home

PART 5 - Special Recognition

Navaho & Native American Code Talkers

(EDITOR'S NOTE: The role of Indigenous American people in fighting of our wars is not often well known. We hope this will help shed a little light on these often-forgotten American heroes. See Wilkipedia)

WWI:

Choctaw tribe and other Native American tribes of Indigenous peoples transmitted phone messages in their tribal tongue assisting the US Army in several battle victories. More than 12,000 American Indian males (nearly 25% of the population at the time served in this war.)

WWII:

The Native American population was less than 350,000 yet and estimated 44,000 American Indian men and women served our country. Despite the dark and painfully endured history, many served out of a sense of patriotism. For others, the military offered economic and educational opportunities as well as world travel. Beginning in 1940 the American military actively recruited Comanches, Choctaws, Hopis, Cherokees, and others to transmit top secret military messages.

Perhaps most well know were the Navajo Code Talkers recruited by the Marines in 1941-42. Philip Johnson was a WWI veteran who had heard about the success of the Choctaw telephone squad. Although not himself native American, he had grown up on a reservation and suggested to the Marine Corps that Navajos and other tribes could be used in maintaining communications secrets. After seeing some demonstration, the Marine Corps were so impressed they began recruiting Navajos to develop a secret code within their language.

Many Code Talkers went on to earn medals such as Purple Hearts, Silver Stars, Good Conduct Medals, and Combat Infantry Badges during and after the war. But due to its secret classification, it would take nearly 40 years before the Code Talkers got Special recognition. Finally, in 2000 the United States Congress passed legislation to honor the Navajo Code Talkers and gave them special gold and silver Congressional Medals. And in 2001 the following Presidential recognition:

'Gentlemen, your service inspires the respect and admiration of all Americans, and our gratitude is expressed for all time, in the medals it is now my honor to present'-

President George W. Bush (The White House, Washington, D.C.)

(Notes: See AmericanIndian.si.edu)

The Underground Resistance

EDITOR'S NOTE:

In WWII the civilian underground fighters in France and virtually every country came to be also known as *'The Resistance.'* I heard a story of a town which was situated on the Northern part of France known as wine country. There was a large Church in town and up on the hill was a small Chapel. There was also hidden a long five-mile underground tunnel built by the Romans nearly 2000 years ago! Its opening was covered by a moveable rotating stone wall, which the Germans fortunately never discovered! This allowed the underground freedom fighters a significant advantage of surprise and secrecy in their attacks against Nazi occupation troops, throughout this particular village during the war until allied liberation in 1944. It is noted that even today people do not want to share these often painful memories in a public manner.

Tribute to Italian Americans and the Columbus Memorial Fund of 1945

EDITOR'S Note: At the time of this publication, *"War Stories & Remembrance"* has been able to secure permission from two families to republish names of these two individuals to remember their sacrifices as young Italian-Americans fulfilling their patriotic duty to God and country. Their stories were so compelling, especially in light of the anarchistic days we now find ourselves in, this editor wanted to at least acknowledge their great sacrifices on behalf of our country.

Rev Johnny Cardamone
June 23, 2020

My late Maternal Sicilian Grandmother Beatrice Scianna Marino immigrated along with her 8 brothers from Palermo around 1910 to the area of Fairfield county Connecticut. She eventually met and married, Filippo Marino, a barber in South Norwalk who came from

Marsala, Sicily, arriving here October 12, 1907.

My paternal grandfather, Vincenzo Cardamone, came with his brother Dominick in 1908, settling in Scranton Pennsylvania as coal miners, where he would eventually meet and marry my grandmother Mary Apa Cardamone, who inspired this book.

Like most immigrants throughout our American history, they were often met with prejudice and suspicion. The Italian and Sicilian immigrants carried by association the stigma of the Mafia from the old country, and elements of that organized crime followed them to American cities. So much so that there was often a prevailing attitude of prejudice and suspicion which questioned the loyalties of these new Italian immigrants. Many believe in some ways these questions were not fully settled in the minds of average White Americans until the end of WWII. As Italian Americans proved their love and loyalty for our great Country, by the sacrifice of their son's blood on foreign soil, even on their old country Italian soil.

At the time of this writing there is presently taking place a debate over statues of what previous generations deemed 'Heros'. Christopher Columbus for 500 years has been a source of Italian American pride for his courage as an early European explorer, of what would later be recognized by another Italian explorer, Amerigo Vespucci, as the New World. Recently (June 2020) Columbus's statue was removed from the Heritage Wall in my hometown of Norwalk, Connecticut. This has been a cause of great distress to many proud Italian Americans and at this writing is a source of much soul searching.

(EDITOR'S NOTE: Even though the King of Italy was perhaps too cheap to pay for the voyage, Columbus found favor with King Ferdinand and Queen Isabella of Spain, otherwise we might all be speaking Italian!)

In this day of revisionist history, we must not shy away from the dark aspects of this history, and the suffering of Native peoples in the what Europeans would call the New World. (See the powerful scene at the end of the film 'Apocalypto' by Mel Gibson). Remembering the Spaniard conquistadors, despite perhaps their own motivation of greed, a vice found unfortunately in most humans, found some of these ancient peoples like the Aztecs who were observed to have practiced things like human sacrifice! Something which came to an end as the New World was Christianized, though it was sadly replaced by the scourge of slavery. But let us not fear pulling back the curtain of our past but tell it's Truth, warts and all and learn as we strive to 'right the wrongs' and become One people, and form what our fore fathers called, a more perfect Union.

Rev. J.P.C.

COLUMBUS DAY REMEMBRANCE

Columbus statue removed from Heritage Wall Norwalk, CT June 2020.
It's whereabouts is unknown.

The following is taken from a Non-copyrighted event booklet from 1945 in which my grandma Bea Marino attended, no doubt with many of her friends and neighbors.

Program cover From October 12, 1945 from Columbus Memorial Fund, Italian American War Tribute program. Right: Inside of program with notes from my Sicilian grandmother Beatrice Scianna Marino

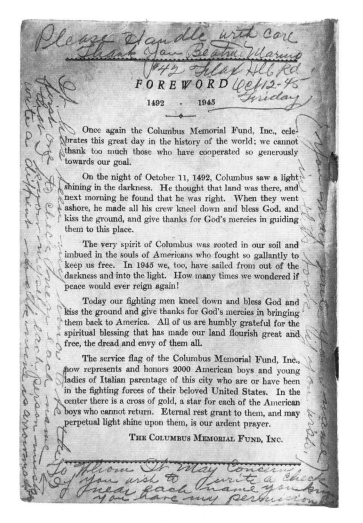

Sergeant John Basilone, Congressional Medal of Honor:

SERGEANT JOHN BASILONE

Sgt. Basilone was the first enlisted Marine of World War II to receive the Congressional Medal of Honor. He refused a commission, electing to return to his battalion in the Pacific area. He gave his life in the hard, bitter struggle for Iwo Jima.

We honor and revere the memory of Sgt. Basilone, who became our friend by his modest, unassuming manner at our banquet in 1943.

Columbus Memorial Fund, Inc.

We could not secure permission to use the photo of Sergeant John Basilone but wanted to at least offer this recognition.

Italian-American Heros of WWII

Michael P. Abruscato

PRIVATE MICHAEL P. ABRUSCATO, 26, husband of Mrs. Barbara Bogart Abruscato, 12 Byington Place, and son of Mr. and Mrs. Joseph Abruscato of 13 Donovan St., entered service in May, 1944. He trained at Camp Blanding, Fla., and went overseas in November, 1944, with the 34th Division.

Pvt. Abruscato wrote his wife on April 10, 1945, that in two weeks he was to enter OCS School in Italy. Shortly thereafter, word was received that he had been killed in action on April 18, 1945. Besides his wife, Pvt. Abruscato is also survived by a young daughter, Michele.

Sponsored by Dr. Felix Cifatte

On August 7, 2020 I attended a meeting held at the Word Alive Bible Church in Norwalk which was sponsored by Jeffrey Dewitt and The Military order of the Purple Heart. It was a tremendous honor to meet many members of what we call our 'Gold Star' families. There I met Pvt. Abruscato's daughter Michele, his nephew Joe, as well as his remaining and youngest of nine siblings sister Dorothy age 99! (Photo used with their permission)

Liberty Tremonte

(EDITOR'S NOTE: I personally interviewed someone who grew up in the Italian section of Westport known as Saugatuck where the Trem-

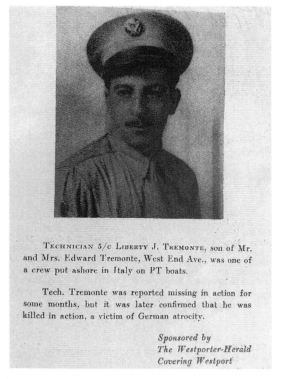

TECHNICIAN 5/c LIBERTY J. TREMONTE, son of Mr.
and Mrs. Edward Tremonte, West End Ave., was one of
a crew put ashore in Italy on PT boats.

Tech. Tremonte was reported missing in action for
some months, but it was later confirmed that he was
killed in action, a victim of German atrocity.

Sponsored by
The Westporter-Herald
Covering Westport

onte family lived. My uncle Frank's cousin said when Mrs Tremonte received the news of her son's death during the War in Italy, that her screams could be heard all over town. A terrible heartbreakingly sad reminder of the price our Gold Star families have paid. Liberty Tremonte spoke Italian and was on a special mission when they were captured by the Germans. Accused as spies the German soldiers did not want to execute them, as they were captured in uniform and should have been afforded protection under the Geneva convention. But a higher up general gave the orders, and so as not to arouse suspicion in the Italian village where they were held, instead of being shot, they were bludgeoned to death with rifle butts, and it was reported at least two men were buried alive. Hence why the above caption describes his death as a victim of German atrocity. A telegram would arrive days later with orders to stay the executions, alas too late. The Nazi general who had given the original order for execution was eventually tried at Nuremberg after the War and executed himself by the Allies.)

We extend much appreciation for the following notes which are from nephew Joseph Tremonte, and used with his permission for this publication.

"Here are the final resting places for my Uncle Liberty Tremonte's unit:"

Just like the medals that had been shining during the years of re-conquered peace. The "Silver Star" and "Purple Heart" were awarded to all the "fifteen men of the mission:

Sgt De Flumeri,

Sgt Vieceli,

T/5 Tremonte (also awarded the "Bronze Arrowhead"),

T/5 Sirico,

T/5 Leone,

T/5 Libardi,

T/5 Squatrito rest in the Florence American Cemetery;

Sgt Noia and Lt Traficante in the Calvary Cemetery in Woodside, NY;

Lt Russo in the Immaculate Conception Cemetery of Upper Montclair, NJ,

T/5 Mauro in St John's Cemetery in Middle Village NY,

T/5 Calcara in Mazara del Vallo and a park in Detroit is dedicated to him,

T/5 Farrell (also awarded the Bronze Arrowhead) in St. Thomas' Cemetery in Fairfield Connecticut,

T/5 Di Sclafani in the Cypress Hills Cemetery, NY,

T/5 Savino in the Long Island National Cemetery in East Farmingdale NY.

Liberty Tremonte
Technician Fifth Class, U.S. Army
2677th Company, Office of Strategic Services*
Died: March 26, 1944
Buried at: Plot G Row 11 Grave 28
Florence American Cemetery
Florence, Italy

Awards: Silver Star, Purple Heart

*Office of Strategic Services founded in 1942 and became today's CIA in 1947.

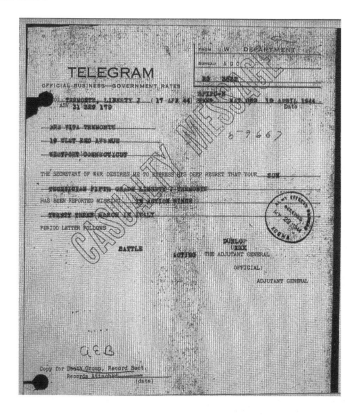

Hello Family,

I believe that it will give us all something to be proud of and think about this Memorial Day.

When you read the Dostler article by Winston G. Ramsey you will see that the German officers did everything they could to get the execution orders reversed. Please see page 10, bottom of the 3rd column. A cable arrived stating that the American soldiers were not to be shot but it arrived too late.

All the best.
Joe Tremonte

The Willow Street Eight of Portchester, NY by Joseph Sabia

(EDITOR'S NOTE):

This editor met Joe Sabia September 2019 at an American Legion celebration in Norwalk Connecticut. The pamphlet that he wrote I found so fascinating that I wanted to at least make reference to it here with the hope that future editions of *War Stories & Remembrance* will be able to publish its full content. Unfortunately, at the time of this publication, *"War Stories & Remembrance"* had not secured such permission from families or news sources in order to republish full names. But the individuals and their sacrifices as young Italian/Americans fulfilling their patriotic duty to God and country was so compelling, that this editor wanted to at least acknowledge their great sacrifices on behalf of our country.

Rev Johnny Cardamone
June 23, 2020

The Willow Street Eight: A Memorial: by Joe Sabia

This pamphlet is intended as a work in progress. It was written in partial fulfillment for an Eagle Scout Project in 2003. It is my sincere hope that anyone having any additional information would please contact the Port Chester Historical Society or the author, Joseph Sabia, directly. (Used with permission)

Lieutenant Alfonse G.-----
Private Dominick C.-----
Staff Sergeant John R-----.
Private Joseph P-----.
Sergeant Daniel L-----.
Private Donato M.-----
Private First Class Orlando G-----.
Corporal Joseph C.-----

Alfonse, Dominick, John, Joseph, Daniel, Donato, Orlando, and Joe all were raised on a tiny dead-end street in Port Chester, New York.

They were all friends who played stickball, kick the can, and ate and congregated at Tiny's Lunch together. All eight attended Roosevelt Elementary School, Port Chester Junior High School, and graduated from Port Chester High School. These eight men along with over a hundred other Port Chester citizens gave their lives in the service of their country during World War II. On May 24, 1992, a plaque was erected in Memorial Park on Westchester Avenue to acknowledge *The Willow Street Eight.* May they Rest In Peace.

END OF WWII:
STUART BADEN: A Boy Remembers

The following is in his own words:

John so good to hear from you. I was a wee babe, during the war, but I do have a memory to share.

World War II ended in the summer of 1945. I was 5 years old. Everyone was very happy, running up and down the streets shouting; "The war is over, the war is over!" I didn't know what a war was, but I realized it must have been a very bad thing, if everyone was so happy that it was over! People were scampering about with all kinds of homemade noisemakers. I myself had a big wooden spoon that I banged against of a metal pot. One creative individual made a great racket by banging 2 garbage can covers together.

My father toasting the war's end with several of his friends, was also very happy that the war was over. It was the only time in my life that I ever saw my father inebriated. (Actually "drunk" would be a more accurate adjective, but I have trouble using the word drunk, with regards to my beloved dad.) My mother on the other hand had no trouble berating him for being DRUNK. Mom was very upset. I guess her disdain for dad's toasting outdid her happiness that the war was over. It was the only time I ever witnessed a quarrel between my parents. Actually "fight" would be a more accurate noun, but I have trouble using the word fight, with regards to my beloved parents.

Of course, for so many reasons it is a night I can still recall with great clarity. The night ended with more celebration, outside the house, and my dad sleeping on the couch.

KOREA – 1950-1954

FORWARD

The Korean War had often been referred to as 'The Forgotten War'. It began on June 25, 1950 when Communist North Korea (with the support of China and the Soviet Union) invaded South Korea (with support of the United Nations and it's main ally the United States). The US lost over 36,000 soldiers in the conflict which took approximately 3 million lives, and ended with a truce armistice signed on July 27, 1953. (See Wikipedia).

Years ago my wife and I attended a Billy Graham School of Evangelism conference for pastors in Orlando Florida, circa 1997. While there I had lunch one day with an African American pastor who had been a Korean war veteran. I don't recall his name these years later, but Korea was the first integrated war in which black and white soldiers fought along side each other. He told the story of his platoon being overrun by the enemy. He was wounded severely in the knee and knocked unconscious by an explosion of some kind. As he was coming to he could hear Korean voices around him. It was the enemy. He 'played dead' which in the end saved his life! Once the North Koreans retreated, Americans troops reinforcements returned to rescue the wounded and recover the dead.

Ralph Pagano: Once a Marine Always a Marine

These stories as told to Dave Van Buskirk and this Editor.

Ralphie was born in South Norwalk and grew up off Woodward Ave. His mother Gooma Tesse (Teresa) was best friends with my grandma Bea Marino and was my mother's godmother. My grandpa Philip Marino was his barber. He said my grandparents were very poor and lived in a cold-water flat (upstairs apartment) with no heat. Just a kerosene heater, and no bathroom! A toilet in the closet!

Ralph worked at the Hat factory on Van Zant Street before he was drafted into the Marines at age 18 in 1948. When the Korean war broke out, he was sent overseas. On his 21st birthday he asked for a day off from fighting, but he did not get it. It was cold in Korea and many of the men lost toes, fingers, and even limbs due to the frost bite. They would be out exposed in the woods and wilderness waiting for relief that often came too late.

One time on guard duty his feet were so cold they lit a fire. But this drew the attention of the North Koreans who began to shell them with mortars. They had to choose between frost bite and being bombed. A fire fight ensued for 4-5 hours before reinforcements had come to help. They lost over 60 men. Many times, Ralph could hear and even feel the bullets whizzing over his head. One even went through his hat. He attributed his short stature 5'3" to saving his life!

Ralph said they also fought alongside the Turks who he said were good fighters. He said we would have won the war and we were beating the North Koreans until the Chinese came in. During the daytime it was like camping out with your buddies and they had fun. But at night the Chinese army would attack coming over the hills in throngs and the Americans would just mow them down with withering machine gun fire.

Ralph came home on leave for Christmas and his mother asked my grandma if Annie my Mom would go to the movies with Ralph. She said yes but told Ralph it was nothing serious because she was engaged at the time to Billy Toth who was also away in the service. Ralph said they walked down to the Rialto theater. He also had some good times on furlough in Japan as the GIs would walk down the streets of Tokyo and meet the Japanese people, who we were now friends with having just finished WWII five years earlier.

Opon returning home he met and married the love of his life Ann and they raised two wonderful children while Ralph worked for the City of Norwalk DPW. He loved baseball and we all remember him coaching and umpiring the Babe Ruth league at Nathan Hale school right behind where he lived.

He and his wife loved to travel especially to Las Vegas where I think he said they visited nearly 40 times! They also loved Atlantic City and use to stay at Mrs. Trumps hotel. They said she was very friendly and a gracious host.

After losing his wife of many years, Ralph was often lonely and many times during the week would stop by the bank where Dave and I worked to visit. He loved being a Marine and wore his veterans hat proudly till the day he died April 2019. We will miss him. Semper Fi!

*Left to right from top: Happy wedding day to Ann the love of his life; Relaxing at mama's.
Ralphs military paraphnelia; Always a proud grandpa; And a proud marine!
Saying goodbye. A proud nation honors her dead. And says, thank you!*

Charles Batterson: Army Medic

War Memories shared by his son Robert and daughter Carol Ann.

One day while my Dad and I were talking; It was at the start of the COVID-19 pandemic. He said: I'll tell you what my commander said to us before we went into battle. "They can get some of us, but they can't get all of us."

Dad volunteered for the Army and went into service on 3/24/1952, during the Korean War. He was part of the 1666 Med Co 9th Inf Regt.

Dad didn't choose to be a Combat Medic in the Army. They chose him. An army official came to him and said: you're going to go for 4 weeks training and will become a Combat Medic. Dad said No, I don't want to. He was told Yes, you are. He said he wasn't sure what they saw in him that they had chosen him to be a Medic—a position of such importance.

When he was a Combat Medic in the Korean War, he said the wounded soldiers he cared for thought he was a real doctor. He didn't let them know he only had a few weeks training. When he left the Army he was a grade/rank: CPL (T) 20. According to his discharge papers he received two bronze stars, but he never talked about them and we never saw them.

He was a plumber before going into the Army and returned to the plumbing trade on his return home and eventually started his own business, *Batterson Plumbing & Heating.*

One of the things Dad wanted was to be buried with his Combat Medic Badge.

(Picture below.)

EDITOR NOTE: It contains at least five significant elements of symbolism:

First, it is the International Medical symbol of the serpents on the staff, (Taken from the Old Testament in book of Numbers 21:9, Gospel of John 3:14) the Cross a sign of healing. The stretcher for carrying and caring for the wounded; The crown of laurel for victory, and the guardian angels wings for protection.

Left to right from top: Combat Medic Badge; Shipping out with Buddies for Korea; Charlie in the hill country of Korea. Charlie in uniform. Charlie in front with the gang. Charlie and my aunt Lucille they loved the beach.

'Bert': An Anonymous Black Soldier's Experience

(EDITOR) A_____told me these stories when I interviewed him on several occasions.

He was born Colored as it was called, on a tobacco farm in rural North Carolina in 1928. Mother gave him up as a baby to an older couple.

His Step father: (Black) born a slave in 1855

His Step mother: (White) born 1865

He grew up and played football in school. He told me the kids used to go up to the mountain on Saturday night, to get into 'mischief'. He said I stayed at the drug store and sat on the Royal cola machine and stayed away from the girls, and trouble!

He used to say, 'I knew my place,' having grown up in the south in the 1930s and 40s with segregation. But he also would say, 'I had my day in the sun too!' We will leave it at that.

He got into some trouble one day doing some mischief behind the store, getting into something but he said, this nice white man, I believe a banker, looked out for me and helped me.

When I would ask him repeatedly, he would say, I did not experience much racism; I got along with everybody. (He always had a positive attitude, and this is how he remembers his life, even at our last interview in January 2020, with no bitterness.)

Went into the US Army sent to Korea.

He told me this story:

'One night I was on guard duty. When suddenly out of nowhere, this fellow comes walking along. Turned out he ended up being a North Korean General! He spoke better English than I did! He had gone to school in the states in years previous. The war was winding down and he was walking back north to his home. I told him, I don't have nothing against you. I didn't want to be here either, I was playing football in school when they called me and sent me over here. He offered me his gold sword! I said if I keep it, they, meaning my US officers, will just take it away from me at the base. I sent him on his way back home.

When we would go on leave to Japan, I met a nice lady. She was widowed and had to make a living. We would see each other whenever I was on leave. The second time or so I visited, I heard a little noise. Out from behind the sofa a little face appeared. And then another, and another! Turned out she had four kids! They were trained to be quiet. I believe she had lost her husband during Japans defeat in WWII.

I seriously thought about marrying her. But in the end, our lives were worlds away, and though our paths crossed for this short time, I guess it was not in our destiny to remain together.

EDITOR'S NOTE:

The US ARMY can serve as Goodwill Ambassadors: There is much good our country has accomplished in spite of the tragic events that war brings with it. The country of South Korea is a good example.

Years ago, I heard Pastor Bill Hybels telling the story of Bill Pierce the founder of World Vision, who as a young man was doing missions

The poor children of Korea 1954

work in Korea after the war around 1954. He said there was a food line of children patiently waiting for handout of a meal. He said the children began to drop from the hunger and tragically die on the spot. He hurried to the front of the line and the women in charge simply said, 'There is no more food.' When he was returning to the states a missionary woman there challenged him to send her $5 every month and she would see that children would be fed. And so were these humble beginnings of what would go on to become, one of the largest Evangelical Christian mission organizations in the world, which has helped countless millions with relief, food, and education.

Simple thatched homes of Korea 1954. Korean veteran's personal photo's used with permission

Chapter 4

VIETNAM – 1962-1975

FOREWORD

Perhaps no war since the Civil War has divided our country more than the war in Vietnam. Like many overseas conflicts Americans by and large probably did not even know it's where abouts on a map, let alone much of its history. The US deployed 2.7 million soldiers and lost over 58,000 troops with a total of over 1.2 million combatant deaths. (see Wikipedia). After the US left Vietnam in 1975 the communist Khmer Rogue are estimated to have killed more than 2 million civilians.

I visited the Vietnam Memorial in Washington DC, a very moving tribute, when it opened around November of 1982. There is also *'The Three Soldiers'* a bronze statue by Frederick Hart dedicated on Veterans day November 11, 1984 as part of the Vietnam Veterans Memorial. It is said to be the first representation of and African-American on the National Mall (See Wikipedia)

While in Bible college in that late 1970's my roommate had me read the 1958 political novel, *'The Ugly American.'* I often thought if more Americans had read this, perhaps we would have never entered Vietnam.

Ed Consolati: Navy USS Independence

DATE ENLISTED & BRANCH OF SERVICE: January 29, 1964 to January 21, 1966. U.S. Navy.

BASIC TRAINING: Great Lakes Chicago, Eight weeks, Naval Station

THEATER OF OPERATIONS: Gulf of Tonkin, Yankee Station.

MOST MEMORABLE EXPERIENCE:

When the U.S.S. Enterprise, relieved us in December 1965, I will never forget the two largest war ships in the world side by side! The Independence was the flagship at that time, high level meetings were held at this ship. General Westmorland was walking through the mess deck and stopped under an air conditioner vent. He asked a nearby sailor, "Is it always like this?" Other dignitaries Secretary of defense McNamara, Nguyn Casky Prime Minister of South Vietnam, also came aboard for high level meetings.

During the bombing runs and when the pilots would return, I would go up to the fan tail and hope and pray they would have a safe landing, I did this quite often as my bunk was just below the fantail. Many years later I took my children to the Air Force museum in Washington DC. There I spotted an area that was for aircraft carriers, and I came across a fantail from the USS Independence. I shed a tear.

The Independence (CV 17-62), made history in May 1965 where she steamed across the Atlantic ocean, around South Africa and through the Indian ocean to the south China sea to assume duties with the 7th fleet. The ship departed from the 6th feet from Norfolk Virginia. The Independence was a beautiful well-run ship. The crew from the green stripe flight decker's, to the red machinists' mates, to the white bosn mates, supply and to the galley which served good food 23 hours a day!

Another memory is the skillfulness of the pilots landing on the flight deck! This feat is one of the most dangerous accomplishments ever in the world! No matter how talented these pilots are, the first signal they did often after landing was to give the thumbs up sign to the flight deck crew!

MOST FRIGHTENING SITUATIONS:

When the Captain announced General Quarters and said, "This is no drill." Lasted about two hours a pre-cautionary event.

YOUR VIEW OF GOD & FAITH IN THE MIDST OF WAR:

I depended on my faith and God that no sailor or pilot would get injured. Also, that no pilot would get killed or captured.

HOW YOU WERE CHANGED BY YOUR EXPERIENCE?

It changed me in a way to show more compassion for people.

THE IMPACT ON YOUR FUTURE & CAREER:

The impact on my life made me want to do the best I possibly can. Being interested in the outdoors, I took up agronomy at the School of Stockbridge UMASS and managed a golf course for 43 years.

SOME FUNNY MEMORIES AFTER SERVICE:

When I was discharged in January 1966, I sent my sea bag home to my parents in Massachusetts. I decided to stay in Maryland checking out a job opportunity but got sidetracked and stayed for a couple of days. My sea bag got home before I did! Mom wasn't too happy when that happened as you can imagine what went through her mind. But of course she and dad were happy finally to have me home.

YOUR VIEW ON THIS PRESENT GENERATION & OUR COUNTRY'S DIRECTION:

I guess I'm old fashioned but it scares me as I go by schools, to see students boys and girls; 10, 11, 12 years old with orange and freestyle hair. The parents are to blame for this.

LIFE ON THE HOME FRONT:

Life has been generous to me, a great wife and three wonderful kids; All college educated. Thank God!

USS Independence on maneuvers; Edward Consolati, age 22; Edward Consolati on left and buddies share a navy beverage.

Dave Zavory: US Army

BASIC TRAINING: Fort Dix, N.J. A.I. T. Fort Polk, LA
THEATER OF OPERATIONS: Republic of Vietnam June 1968-June 1969

WAR AND BATTLE EXPERIENCES

As a young man of 18 upon graduating from Norwalk High school, I went to work for the Union as a dump truck driver making good money, or so I thought. But I had a cloud hovering over me knowing that in a short time I would be drafted. It was a time of anxiety and apprehension among late teen males. The war in Vietnam was escalating rapidly and then President Johnson wanted more troops overseas. As the second son of a WWII veteran, who still had shrapnel near his heart, I felt it was my duty to let the Army use my services.

Already at that time many people began realizing or perceiving that this war was different in the way it was being executed. The way our leaders were dealing with it was not right or supported by much of the country. Blindly I accepted the fact that if Uncle Sam needs you, then your attitude is, "Let's Go! So as of January 1968, I became the property of Uncle Sam S-NU552724279 was my dog tag number. My basic training was at Ft Dix New Jersey for eight weeks.

Training for Advanced Infantry Training A. I. T. was at fort Polk Louisiana. Hell, I knew I was going to Vietnam! So here was the glitch. I was engaged to a lovely girl, and the dilemma was do I get married before shipping out or not? Happily, she planned a lovely wedding in just 8 weeks, and after Two and a half weeks of marriage I was off to Vietnam! After the wedding that was a first-class low point.

Upon arrival in Vietnam, as the 707 jet was descending, lights were extinguished and all aboard were wondering, 'Will we get shot at?' After the uneventful landing we were assigned to 'Replacement Company'. Then after several days I was assigned to a unit: American Division 198th Infantry Brigade 5th Battalion, 46th Infantry, C Company. As an infantry rifleman the M-16 was the weapon of Choice.

Upon arrival in my unit, I was welcomed by most and taken under their wings. Obviously the first ride on helicopters was exciting yet scared your ass off too! Fortunately, it was uneventful. After several months, the friendship bonds made were as strong as steel and when buddies went home after fulfilling their tour of 12 months, it was sad to see them leave. When a buddy was wounded or killed, it was a devastating thing to experience. Sadly, I did witness soldiers that I was closer to than others get wounded and two weeks before I came home, one man who actually did get killed.

Things that were going on back in the States were disheartening to me. In the summer of 1968 we had just experienced the assassination of MLK and Bobby Kennedy and now it was the Democratic convention in Chicago, Riots, Hippies, things like that at the time that seemed detrimental to our way of life, that we were accustomed to. While in Vietnam, my beloved Church Pastor, Rev. John Butosi, would mail church newsletters and Sunday bulletins to me. I so looked forward to receiving them and after returning home unscathed, this helped cement my faith in God.

Upon returning home, my perception of the war changed. I so believed that what my fellow soldiers and I did was "The right thing to do." But at home in 1969, hearing the politicians and the protesters began to shed some doubt.

A specific incident occurred there that was quite impacting. When I first arrived in my unit obviously being the 'New Guy', I was awarded garbage detail. We would empty all of the 55-gallon garbage drums from the mess hall into a 2 ½ ton truck and take it to a pit outside of the perimeter of the base where we were stationed. As soon as we dumped it, the Vietnamese children in the village would come and collect the scraps of food for their sustenance. How humbling that was! It sure gave me a greater appreciation for all we had at home. Once home, my outlook on life changed. Until Vietnam, I never realized how privileged and blessed we are in America. Listening to people complain about so many mundane things truly irked me!

The last six months of my Army obligation I spent at Fort Lewis, Washington. I was assigned to a training unit. By then I had my wife with me, and we became friends with two other couples. All of us were in the same boat, with our military life and made the most of it.

MOST MEMORABLE EXPERIENCE: Stepping on a "Bouncing Betty" land mine, having it shoot up chest high but Not detonate! (04/11/1969)

MOST FRIGHTENING SITUATIONS: When on the perimeter at 2:00 am and being probed or attacked by the VC (Viet Cong).

SOME FUNNY MEMORIES:

Our understaffed platoon was the last group of 28 men on a fire base which was being dismantled and abandoned. Somehow the re-supply helicopter mistakenly left us a case of 12 dozen eggs! We had no cooking facility there or utensils! But we did have a vehicle with hubcaps, so we washed out several hubcaps and cooked the eggs in them! Now that's Army resourcefulness!

(EDITOR'S NOTE: I was ten years old when my 'cousin' Dave left for Vietnam. (his wife Joanne's mother, Henrietta was first cousin to my Mom, Annie Marino) In my young naïve mind I thought of it as an exciting camping adventure. To this day if I hear the song by Burt Bacharach and sung by Diane Warwick, *"I Say a Little Prayer for You,"* it brings me back to those years, when we prayed for his safe return.

Left to right from top: SAYING GOOD BYE; Getting the A Salute! From his dad and new father-in-law and the Italian Uncle's at the American Legion, Almost all were WWII Vets; This is where it starts to set in and feel real! Certificate of Training; A Proud brother and father flank an excited Dave.

Left to right from top: A Proud family, Dad, wife Joanne, and Mom; Norwalk Hour News paper; That is what is was All about; The man and his uniform! A Last kiss goodbye (EDITOR'S NOTE: I always cry when I see this photo)

Saying hello to Vietnam; Arms for war & helicoptors

*On patrols & camping out in the back country; Starting to experience the fatigue of war &
missing home; Vietnamese civilians & kids, captured Viet-Cong prisoners*

Left to right from top: Second honeymoon in Hawaii! My sweet wife Joanne met me there: having some R&R; USO shows and then back home. We are still looking for Bob Hope! Vietnamese jazz band & dancers! (EDITOR'S NOTE: Upon arriving home the fun ended so to speak. The years 1968-69 had been a time of tremendous turmoil in the USA. And it seems as of this writing today June 2020, sadly, not as much has changed as we had hoped)

Howard Williams: US Navy

IMPACT OF WAR ON PEOPLES LIVES: My experiences
Howard Williams, Chief Petty Officer, ISC, USN-R Retired
Brief background:

Active duty in the Western Pacific during mid-60's. Bulk of service in Naval Reserve; total 26 years. 1965-1991. BSBM degree. Retired Manufacturing Quality Engineer.

War has shown me the good and bad side of the human race. A species quite capable of either. To me nothing has fundamentally changed since the first cave man threw the first rock at another cave man in anger. (The ... "you have resources I want. We share/negotiate or, if necessary; fight for it" ...philosophy). What has changed is the technology. In the distant-past, a few hundred people killed in any one given battle had no significant effect on the planet. With today's technology, we could destroy the planet, via Nuclear/Biological/Chemical, (NBC) warfare. This worries me. Especially terrorist and/or rogue regime setting-off some sort of perfect storm chain-reaction.

There are two individuals whom I especially admire: Albert Einstein and Admiral Hyman Rickover (father of the Nuclear Navy). Both believed in the human spirit but questioned our future as to how we manage our advancing technology. Like fire, used for good or bad.

Some quotes:

Rickover: "Optimism and stupidity are almost synonymous". "Faith alone will not sustain us." "It is not important what religion a man follows. What IS important is that he lives-up to its values."

Einstein: "Science without Religion is lame. Religion without Science is blind." "I don't know what weapons will be used in WW-3 but WW-4 will be fought with sticks and stones."

One more: Emily Dickinson (daughter of a strict Calvinist Minister): "Faith is a fine invention when gentlemen can see, but microscopes are more prudent in an emergency."

Enough philosophy. Some of my own experiences when the Vietnam War was on:

In the western Pacific aboard a San Diego-based repair ship, we made deployments to Hawaii, Japan, Hong Kong, Taiwan and The Philippines. We were a big ship with a 600-man crew. In each port, we serviced/repaired much smaller combatant ships, mostly destroyers. Having a small but complete medical department ("Sick Bay" in Navy Jargon), we occasionally took aboard badly wounded Marines; temporarily-for-transfer. It was appalling ...seeing young America 'kids' 19-20 years old, severely maimed by Vietnamese land mines, "Punji Sticks" ... camouflaged sharp bamboo sticks coated with infectious bull urine and other nasty booby-traps. Legs, arms, hands, blown-off, half a face blown off; you name it. Yet their spirits were high... because they were alive and going home.

In Hong Kong for 7-days of R&R; we swung at anchor mid-harbor. Contracted Chinese garbage barges came to our stern (back of the ship) after each meal; right under our two garbage chutes. Our mess cooks (Navy jargon for kitchen servers), would lug trash cans full of ship's meals leftovers to the chutes. I was at first appalled to see many Chinese "bum-boats" congregate around the barges; their 24/7 residents (many children) with tin cans clamoring for our garbage to just survive! Though instructed not to; some of our crew would sneak an apple from the mess decks and throw it overboard, delighting in watching a bunch of bum-boat kids jump into the water to get it. These kids went for anything. I once saw one sailor from one of our machine shops throw over a big steel bolt. Despicable! Hong Kong especially, was two worlds ... "the haves and the have nots." Mostly have-nots. Ashore in Hong Kong, the Philippines; and also, on visits to Tijuana, Mexico; some hounding by beggars, old and young was typical.

On the brighter side, I witnessed many philanthropic endeavors in some places. Many volunteers from my and other in-port Navy ships helped build orphanages, especially in the Philippines. One of our service boats came to the rescue of a stranded South Vietnamese fishing boat, towing her and her very thankful crew to safety.

Later in my Naval Reserve career, I had many drill-weekend opportunities to fly in anti-submarine patrol aircraft as the intelligence observer. Back then (70's-80's,); we had the cold-war "bad guys;" Russian ships and fishing fleets to observe. Flying low and slow; we waved at them (and most) waved back. Some made other "jesters." Lesson learned: people are people…anywhere regardless of governmental disputes.

Especially, during those cold weekends in January or February; flights to Bermuda or Key West were real "arm-twisters." Sometimes flying "low and slow" just off the Florida beaches; not looking at ships; rather looking at bikini-clad college girls on spring- break!! (Isn't Navy life tough at times?)

All-in-all, my military experiences were a lesson in humanity. War is never the answer. Unfortunately, others don't see it that way. We must be fully prepared to deter it. The human race must learn to work together. Only time will tell.

Clyde 'Jimmy' Jones: US Army

WAR STORIES AND LIFE MEMORIES & EXPERIENCES:

Interviewed on Thursday, July 9, 2020. Q = Question from Editor. J= Jimmy in his own words

I'm with Jimmy Jones, Vietnam veteran Army over here in Norwalk, and he's going to share some of his stories. He just was telling me about his nicknames in Vietnam. Okay Jimmy, tell me about where you were born, growing up and when you went in the service.

I was born in 1950, in a small-town Greensburg, Pennsylvania. It was very rural, a lot of farms. When I became 18 I got out of school and there was no work to be had in the Pittsburgh area because that was a steel mill city, and the steel mills were closing down. So it was a bad time and there were not many jobs around. So, I decided to go into the service. A lot of people were getting drafted and going to Vietnam, but I enlisted for three years; when you're drafted it is only two, and I enlisted for three. I just wanted to be a paratrooper; I didn't care where I went I just signed up as "airborne unassigned." It was 1968.

I went to boot camp in fort Jackson South Carolina. That is when I realized this isn't going to be fun, but I made it through boot camp. And I had signed up to be a paratrooper, so after I believe it was the eight weeks of boot camp, I went to Fort Benning Georgia, that was a jump school. And it was intense physically and mentally because they are trying to prepare you for the worst.

But, on my second jump I landed wrong because the winds were crazy and my ankle swelled up so bad it actually split the boot out, the leather of the boot; we had jump boots on.

And I had to make three more jumps that week, plus the five mile runs in the morning and I had to do that in order to get home for Christmas, because it was so close to Christmas holiday. And I did it, a lot of pain but I did it. After that I went to school for medical supply and after that school, I ended up going to Okinawa for a year.

And over there I was with the first special forces group in Sukarin, Okinawa.

I was there for a year and then I had to come home because my grandfather was my legal guardian and he was dying. Back then in the '60s they had missile bases all around Pittsburgh they attached me to a missile base. I had six months left in the army. And I did not like being attached... I was even in my hometown living off both of my grandparents' house, but I hated state side duty so bad, I had six months left and like a fool I volunteered to go to Vietnam! I could've stayed right in my hometown and just finished everything. But no, I was young and crazy, and now I'm old and crazy.

Vietnam was a real trip. I had some issues there, as there was a lot of drugs, everywhere!

Everybody would get in their own little groups at night; you could tell who the drinkers were, who the pot smokers were, who were the heroin users were. Everybody had their own group. It was crazy.

Since I was in medical supply it was my job to have to go south to get supplies. I was in like a MASH unit, and I had to go south to pick up all the medical supplies for the hospital. We were a field hospital, and if we couldn't get a chopper down with supplies, then I had to drive through a couple bad area passes.

It was on Bongson Pass, I forget all their names and they're no good to drive through especially with a truck full of medical supplies with a big red cross on it. What were we thinking?! Then we started getting shot at! I was driving a 3-quarter ton truck. Speed is not one of their main things you worry about at a time like that! And so, I was going as fast as that truck would take us and I had a first lieutenant who was just over from the States. And he says "slow down." I said, "What are you talking about?" He said you're going over the speed limit. I said you?!#%$&... never mind. And so, when I got back, they busted me for disobeying a direct order and they took the round (bullet) out of the back tire!

And then there was one other time, I don't know how to put this. Everybody had their own drinking group like I said. Well in an airborne unit, in a parachute they have the little chute that comes out first and pulls out the big chute. So, the people who drank they sat under the tiny little chute, the people who smoked pot we had the big chute and the other people just hid and did their stuff, you know because it was all needles and stuff.

Q: What chute were you under?

Marijuana. Everybody was doing that even the drinkers, you know Vietnam was a tough place.

Q: Where did they get the drugs?

You are not going to believe this, but we could buy drugs right on our post because they had what were called Arvans. Republic of Vietnam, they were the good guys down south. And they would be on our post working with us. So, with a lot of them, all we had to do was throw the money over the fence, they knew what we wanted, and they threw the 'stuff' back over the fence and that was it! And they were all military South Vietnamese. But that was just one of many places.

They had these opium dens that guys would go to, they said that they went in there they sat down, and Papa-Son fixed up the pipe for them with the opium. You do that and then you go back in the back room for a couple days and chill out; not a place I would want to be.

Q: It's like a scene out of the movie, *The Deer Hunter*.

Yes, yes, I watched that movie once I won't watch it again, that bothered me more than anything.

Q: Was it accurate?

I don't know, I don't think so, but it scared me. I'll watch any Vietnam war movie, but that one I don't know it just got to me, it really terrified me for a while. But another time I was sitting down under the umbrella and there was an E-7 on duty. He was just walking to his barracks and he saw me sitting down there by myself and he thought I was smoking, and I was not. But you're talking about a place where everybody has got their own little homemade chair and we sit under the flag and that was every night. And he saw me down there in the afternoon, I was off duty. And he said I was smoking which I really was not he called in I think it was a CID or whatever, I forget what the agency was. And what he did was he put his hand in the sand and dragged it trying to pick up what he thought I threw down, he picked up about ten big roaches.

But they still fined me $250! I was up for Sergeant they busted me to PFC and thirty days extra duty. And then they asked if I wanted to re-enlist! I mean do they got nerve or what, you know? I said "no thank you." But then I came home and that was worse than being in Vietnam.

Q: What year was that?

June 1971. I came home I flew into Pittsburgh. I was trying to surprise my family, so I took a cab from the airport to this little town where I lived in. (Greenburg) that area, which is a really smaller town. So, I get to the house and I think I paid the driver $150, back then that was a lot of money, but I wanted to surprise my parents.

So, my dad answers the door, first thing he says is, 'What are you doing here?' I said my time is up, I'm done with the army, I did my three years, I'm out. And then he tells me that I can't stay there! He said I don't have room the other kids have all the rooms taken up.

And I said alright, well I sent you home almost $3,000 could I have that? He says "I spent it." And then he still threw me out into the streets. Welcome home. I knew things were wrong when I got off the plane in the airport in Pittsburgh. Seeing all those protesters and stuff.

Q: Tell me about that.

I was a little boy growing up in this town where there was no police department, volunteer fire department. Everybody knew everybody, real small country town and it was wonderful. And to go into this whole mess that I signed up for it was scary. The whole time I was in I didn't know where I would be going next other than volunteering to go to Vietnam. I lucked out getting Okinawa for a year, that was heaven.

But getting back to coming home, my mother was never allowed to be around me. She had to be at least 25 miles away for 21 years because the cops saw my brother and I in a crib, in a bad situation. So, what do they do? They give me and my brother to my dad, who was no bargain either. But that is what went on back then and he just wasn't a person to look up to.

You know I am totally different. I care about people, I like people. But even in my hometown and I was only over there in Vietnam six months. But when I came back, people that I grew up with were strange to me, like I could not understand it I'm just a little country boy and we were being blamed for everything that was wrong in the country. That was hard to take.

Q: That is how people treated returning Vietnam veterans?

Oh God, yeah! I was afraid to go places because of the protesters.

Q: What did you see at the airport?

A bunch of people with the Hari Krishna stuff and I knew that wasn't there when I left; you know. (think George Harrison) and you know you would think someone coming back from a war that people would walk up and say "thank you for your service" or something. Not one! So it was really lonely walking down the halls in the airport, and didn't know what was going on. It was almost like, am I dreaming?

Q: You didn't realize the climate back in the states, you know Martin Luther King had been assassinated, Bobby Kennedy, Vietnam protests.

Yeah, I knew all that. It was sad, I didn't want to believe it and I didn't believe it until I really saw it. But that was tough and then you try to get a job, you don't have any skills because you went in the service right out of high school and people wouldn't hire you. I did a whole bunch of real intense labor jobs, like carrying shingles up to a roof. Back then they didn't have the automatic machines! So I was that automatic machine and that stuff got heavy, those were the kinds of jobs I had to take. So anyhow, when my mother wasn't allowed to be around me, so I never knew her. And so when I was in the army I asked them to help me get in touch with her. I'd like to find who she is where she lives or whatever. And the army did get information and I called her. I said, "I'm going to come up to Connecticut to see you." And that was in '71, and I'm still here. She was originally from Pennsylvania but moved up here, but sadly she was a big drunk.

And so growing up I didn't have many close relationships. Once my stepmother started having children and she didn't want to bother with me or my brother. And me and my brother were responsible for putting food in the house because my dad was drinking and gambling the money away! I was 10 years old I was working in a soda shop loading trucks and my dad made me get a signed receipt from this tiny little soda company to show what I got, just so he could make sure he got it all! Oh, he was no good. Very physically abusive, I was beaten so many times, more than I can count.

Me and my brother would have our bed in the dining room with a pull out couch and if they had people over we had to just go down to the cellar and wait until the company left before we could go to bed.

Q: Was he older or younger?

My brother? He's two years older, four years dumber. But he's a good guy.

Q: Is he in Pennsylvania?

He was in the Navy, but he ended up going to Greece.

Q: What about some of the things that happened in Vietnam to you; what did you see?

One night, here we go with the drugs again. Somebody got 400 hits of purple haze LSD in, so the whole compound was on LSD that night. And we were getting attacked! We were up on the roof partying, listening to music you know. I mean we had speakers that were humongous speakers! (Listening to rock and roll music just like in the movies?) Oh yeah, exactly; and that was fun.

Q: Who were some of the bands you were listening to?

Oh God, Temptations, Motown was big back then in 'Nam and Hendrix there was a variety and you always had the country and western boys over in the corner, you know, under their little chute. There was no way I wanted a hangover in 100-120-degree weather. Not only that everybody got a share of this one job that really sucked.

We had our bathrooms; our luxurious bathrooms were like 20

seats in a row. And if you go in there in the morning, you're sitting down having a conversation with somebody but somebody's got to empty all that stuff. Everybody got a turn you had to empty all those buckets out, dump them in a pit, spray them with kerosene, that was in 120-degree weather and stand there all day stirring it. And they put the place right next to the mess hall. We didn't know if we had pepper or somebody's poop on our food. The military wasn't really bright. That is one we all remembered.

Q: You didn't light it on fire though! I guess the kerosene just supposed to kill the germs!

And they couldn't have hurt that food any more than what it was. It was some nasty stuff.

There would be nights when they call it steak, that was water buffalo. But that's what we had to do.

Q: Did you see any combat there or anything?

No, because I was in the hospital. Well other than being shot at, that was the only thing. But my job was to get the medicine to and from the hospital, so that it's there when the guys come in from the field.

Q: You saw a lot of wounded guys?

Oh God, yeah. I, you know we had to help once the choppers would come in everybody runs out to grab them and they... sometimes if there's heavy casualties, they have to make a decision who's worse. Yeah and that part hurt me, that and taking the personal belongings off of soldiers who were dead. You had to open up the bags and that's the worst thing out of the whole nine yards. That's something I can't forget.

Q: Then that had to be sent to the family?

What they did they brought the wounded to us first. We would try to patch them up the best we could and then fly them down south to Quinon. And after that they process them, they go home. But if they didn't make it, our job was to take off all the personal belongings put them in a bag and put them with the body and that was so hard, I cried so many times. You know I had a heart and to go into something like that, and the only thing I ever shot before was maybe a deer or something; Living near Pittsburgh that's what you did, you know.

And it was sad in these Vietnam villages. We would have to go sometimes downtown to help the community and we'd get a lot of children and that was heart wrenching. Just being down there, I had to be down there to make sure they had what they needed it was also hard being sent down into Bongson. There were so many people that wanted help (civilians in Vietnam? They needed help?) yes, yeah exactly. And to see the kids and what they were like and knowing the poverty and how they lived on dirt floors, I didn't know that there was a part of the world like that! Then I was fortunate enough on my 21st birthday to be in the hospital.

And a friend of mine that I had met Bill Trimmer, he's from Ohio. That's him and I in the photo.

Q: Which is you?

There with the hat on. We just bonded from the war and we didn't really live that far from each other and we just got along so good and to this day we still go to each other's house, he's in Ohio. Or they'll come up here and I'll go down there for the family reunions and everything. It's been a whole 50 years and we're still good friends. (that's good) yeah, I pride my friendships even the ones I have now I've had for 40 something years plus, and that's the people I'm comfortable with.

They're all hard workers they respect me on Veteran's Day, they all call me and say, "thank you" and all the kids call me and say thanks. These kids over here, my neighbors there's two little boys over there; so nice. And they call me Mr. Neighbor and they always tell me on flag day or whatever, they're just so cute. And you know what it makes you feel good.

Q: Yes, do you have kids of your own?

I have a daughter right now who works at the intensive care unit in Yale, and Kaitlyn.

She's only 26. I ask her if she was 33. We were driving in the car one day I asked her "are you 33?" Because she's so mature it just blew my mind. And boy did she put me in my place, "are you really my father?" But she's a sweetheart.

I don't know if you knew that I just had an overdose. (I knew you were in the hospital, but I didn't know) I had broken my back and they had given me medication and I ended up taking a little bit more than I should and almost died! (wow). They took me out of the house my neighbor told me the nurse was saying get moving because we're losing him. I was on a ventilator for three days, and then I went up to a detox in the V.A. at West Haven for a week. And they told me, they said you're not a user, you haven't been a user this is a hiccup in your life. And it was, it was a mistake and I was wrong. But I was looking for relief I was in so much pain.

So, all my friends that I grew up with they're nowhere to be found anymore. I find some, I have this thing classmates from high school in '68 and you can contact people. I've been using that keep them busy.

Q: Let me just ask you as we wrap up the interview the state of things today and the country and the way things are, what is your perspective?

This is not the country that I fought for. I want to point something out to you. (See photo.) We didn't care about color.

Q: what about faith? What about your faith in God?

Oh me and God are tight. I pray every night and during the day.

Q: what about what's going on today, what's changed in the country?

Everything! I don't believe in defacing history. I believe that all lives matter and it sickens me to see these people robbing stores, burning buildings. That's not what its all about you know, doesn't anybody believe in God anymore? You know God pulled me through a lot and I'm not a real religious freak, but I do believe, and I pray every night; I'm bad because I sleep in on Sunday.

Q: Were you raised in any particular church?

United Methodist church in Herminie Pennsylvania. If you think of Hootersville then that's what you got! And that's no lie it was just like that but it was so nice.

Left to right from top: We were All tight like brothers! Heuys were everywhere! Chilling out in Vietnam; Me and my best friend Bill from Ohio; My Buddy Ollie! Jimmy Jones in the back yard; My favorite plaques; Guarding my Flag; My metals

Chapter 5

COLD WAR – 1946-1990
The End of the World as We Knew It

INTRODUCTION

The Cold War is usually considered to span the time from 1947 and the Truman Doctrine until the 1991 dissolution of the Soviet Union (see Wikipedia)

Dominick 'POP' Cardamone, Army, Hawaii, 1946

Pop's story is recorded in his words with the EDITOR'S questions in parenthesis ( ) Done in December 2019. He had just turned 92. My father died May 5, 2020 alone in a nursing home in Sharon Connecticut of the COVID-19. I was able to visit him outside his widow the day before with my son Micah, and we sang to him, 'AMAZING GRACE' his favorite hymn. As of today, we still have not been able to bury him. He is survived by his five children, and his wife of 42 years Helena and step son David Yish. (He was finally buried October 16th.)

Rev. J.P.C., July 6, 2020

I was born in the coal mining town of Scranton, Pennsylvania in 1927. My father Vincenzo (they called him Jimmy) was a coal miner since he came with his brother (Dominick who I was named for) from Calabria Italy in 1908. It was not an easy life. During the Depression there were times we went on Relief or welfare. We used to pick up loose coal along the railroad tracks and bring in home in our wagon to heat the house. You could go to the movies for five cents for a double feature on a Saturday afternoon.

And so, hearing about factory jobs in Connecticut, we moved Memorial Day in 1941 to Norwalk. Goompa Tony and my father and I sat on the back of a truck on a sofa we had roped in. Think of '*The Beverly Hill-Billy's* or the film *'The Grapes of Wrath'* and that is probably what we looked like!

We rented a house on 19 Merwin street, I think the house is gone now. A few years later, I think it was 1944 we were able to buy the old Tierney house on 18 Elm Street. My mother got a job at Meyers pocketbook factory and my father worked for Dan Deering doing road construction, and later on at Nash Engineering doing maintenance. I got a job at Yankee Metal which built automobile mirrors among other things.

(What do you remember about Pearl Harbor?)

It was a big shock my gosh, I was at home on Sunday and we heard it on the radio. So, I ended up down by the theater, and we were getting all the news. And then we all came out of the theater and all the guys had to go to the recruiting station if you were the right age.

I didn't go to school the next day, it was Monday. I listened to the radio and heard *"A day that will live in Infamy."* FDR'S words. Well my cousin Franky was living with us and he got drafted.

(How about the Depression time, you were in Pennsylvania when that came?) Oh yeah, that was bad. I think we ended up on relief. We had to go with the wagon to get a bag of flour and stuff like that, at the store, somewhere because Grandma would bake the homemade bread. (You would use to collect coal?) Grandpa used to go to the dump, we called it the dump in the back of the house. There was a coal mine there years ago, as they threw the stuff out, they made a big pile; and he'd find coal there. And then I would go with my wagon, the house wagon and brought the coal home. And my two sisters would be down in the cellar, I'd dump it there and they had to break up the pieces, so it was smaller. They were Mary and Delina, because Connie and Lucille were too young, I guess. But I had to lug it home on the wagon.

(Once you moved to Connecticut you had oil?) Oil I'm pretty sure. Grandma also had the gas on the stove.

(Did you have chickens?) We got for Easter little chicks and we raised them, and Grandpa built a little coop in the back. Then we ate them. (Did Grandma keep them in the cellar?) There was a guy that would come around with a truck that had live chickens for sale, and she would buy one and keep it in the cellar until Sunday or the Holiday came. Then I held the chicken and she killed it and cut the neck off. Yeah, grab him by the head and cut it off and I'm holding him the wings and the legs. Dip it in the hot water and pull the feathers off. I got a job and did that in a chicken store where they sold live chickens. It was on Commerce street. You had a contraption type thing it would pull the feathers out; it would take it on there and be turning it pulling the feathers out. They would kill them for you and clean it, while you wait. I think it was Falcone's had a place behind St. Mary's Church.

(How about when the war was over, do you remember people coming home?)

Cousin Frankie yeah, Charlie didn't go. Uncle Tony and uncle Carl were Navy; Uncle Frank Anastasia, he was in the Army. He was in the Philippines.

(When did you get drafted?)

It was March 1946. We did our induction at Ft. Devens, Massachusetts and then boot camp at Aberdeen, Maryland. They sent me to a school, where I got my GED because I had left high school like a lot of guys. So, I was in Mechanic school, because I had taken shop at high school, I had some experience with running the lathes.

We then went to Camp Kilmore, New Jersey. Then we took a boat to Honolulu. It was 16 days from New York to Hawaii.

(Did you have any friends with you, anyone from Norwalk?)

No, we're all strangers. Yeah, we got separated, I think it was camp Kilmer, New Jersey, and that's where we got all where we're going to go. (How about Frankie Pastor did he get drafted?) No. (Then Mike Russo, he went later?) Yeah, he did not get drafted when I did. But then after when the Korean War came, he and Ralph Palmer got drafted. I was lucky I didn't have to go to Korea.

(You were in Honolulu?) Yeah, Oahu.

(You were a fireman over there in the Army?) Yeah,

(Were there many fires?) Just one, at the camp there the Captain made a little fire, so we had to put it out.

(Did you see any of the island and did you travel around?) We traveled on the Oahu, they had every Sunday, a tour of the area. And the bus came from our camp, so we got a ride every Sunday and took a tour of different parts of the island.

(Were the people nice over there?) Yeah, yeah.

(Did you meet any nice Hawaiian girls with the grass skirts?)

There were not too many. We were in a base yard and just a little walk out was the city, I forgot the name of it. And there was a drug store there, we used to hang out there. They had the soda fountains years ago, and the we met nice girls there.

(Now what about Pearl Harbor?)

We weren't near there; we were like 20 miles away. Once we landed there then the big base was up the road a piece, inland.

(Did you see any wounded men coming back from the service?)

We were loading dead bodies into coffins. Yeah, they were rattling as you carried them. They brought them in from somewhere, I don't know where.

(Probably from the south Pacific theater?) Yeah, I guess wherever they picked them up; I don't know well they were closed. I don't know how they did it, we just unloaded them. Boats came from the lower islands where they were picking them up and then they ended up in Honolulu. I don't know what they did with them after there, I guess they were sent to cemeteries or back to the states to families to claim and bury or put in military cemeteries.

I spent nine months there; got there in September and left there in May 1947. We took a boat, slow boats to San Francisco. In other words, the Army camped there for a couple days and got processed or whatever. Camp Stoneman, I think. Train took a couple days and nights. Just a regular seat, (A lot of army guys?) No, just a few of us. All the way to New York to get to Grand Central, and then I got a train into South Norwalk. Then the bus, to the bottom of Elm Street. Walked up the street and I was going to surprise my mother. She was on the porch; she just came out to get the mail I guess or something. She smiled and kissed me and was happy I was home.

(So, Jimmy Manzie was friends with you?) Yeah, he lived at the bottom of Merwin street, on Harbor Avenue. Beansie lived down there, it was an Italian neighborhood. Ralphie Tavella had a car and me and Frankie Pastor were hanging out with him one night. It was Annie, Lois and Pinky and us three guys. And that's where we all met and got to know each other, over at Overton's in East Norwalk. (Pinky graduated too with mommy?) Yeah, Pinky and Lois too. (Lois ended up marrying Frankie Pastor?) Right, (Pinky ended up marrying Carmine, my godparents).

(When did you start at C.R. Gibson's?) I don't know what happened at Yankee metal and there was somebody else involved with Gibson's. I don't know, can't remember who it was we both went there to Gibson's asking for a job. Yeah, and then I got hired I don't think he did, and Ralph worked there. (Cousin Henrietta worked at Gibson's with Chault?) They were on the night shift; they had a night shift at Gibson's. (You used to run the stockroom?) I started in the ship room packing orders and we had just come back, and there were no orders to pack in the shipping room. So, they sent me and somebody else in the stock room to take orders and get started. Then I said can I stay here, there was a girl that was running stock and I said I'll run it someday. I took it over I don't know if she got married or she left. And then I ran the stock room.

(Do you remember when they dropped the bomb?) Hiroshima, then Nagasaki. They had to do it Japan wouldn't surrender, then they

did the second one and they finally gave in. But they had killed innocent people, that's war you got to do it.

(What about the violence today?) It's bad, I don't know I can't answer that. (Say a little prayer). Yeah that's about all you can do, hope
God helps us straighten it out.

*Left to right from top: THEATER OF OPERATIONS: Honolulu; Pop in Uniform; Pop in
Fire Truck; Pop; U.S.O. Club; Some buddies who signed scraps of paper.
Where are they now?*

Raymond Gentry, Air Force Greenland, 1947

As told by his wife, Beverly B. Gentry.

Back then I think even after the war the country still needed young men for the service. I know Raymond volunteered because he could go into the service as soon as he was 18. At the time he was living with his grandfather on a tobacco farm in North Carolina. He did not want to go to school, so he quit school the day he turned 18 and he left North Carolina and went back to Chantilly, Virginia to the family farm. Within a week or two he joined the Air Force that was in June of 1947. He went into basic training down south I do not recall where, and after that they sent him to Massachusetts for a few months of more training and preparation. From there he went to Greenland. The officers were kidding him, and they told him he'd love it in Greenland because there was a woman behind every tree! But when he got to Greenland, there weren't no trees!

So that was not true. But he played a lot of poker that year and would send his money home and his mother saved it for him. He spent a year there in Greenland and then he came to Mobile, Alabama where he was stationed at the Brookley air base. And that is when I met him one night at a dance. He winked at me across the floor, so I winked back! (For more details see her book "My Life with Raymond"). I only went with him for six months and then we were married in September 1949. He remained stationed there at Brookley Air Force base in Mobile. Pensacola Florida nearby was the Navy base.

It was after the war was over, so he did not do much in the service. He did make one promotion and he made from a private to a corporal. He worked in parts department and was learning mechanics. He would drive a jeep on Brookley, on the base and delivered parts for the airplanes to the mechanics and supplies. And every now and then he would take that jeep and come to my house. He was not supposed to take it off the base, but he did. He would do things like that.

His three years would be up in June of 1950. He did not want to re-enlist, but I did want him to re-enlist, but he chose not to. We had to go to Virginia, and he got out of the service the first week of June 1950.

And as it turned out within less than two weeks the Korean war started! So, if his release date had been another week, he would not have been able to get out of the service because of the Korean war. Well, I guess for his sake it's a good thing he didn't listen to me because I didn't know the Korean war was going to break out. So, it did keep him out of the war time.

He got some benefits for being in the service three years. They gave him $1,000 worth of mechanical tools to work with and payed him $90 a month. Plus, he worked for his mother and stepfather and learned to be a mechanic, which became his lifelong trade and vocation, and he was a good mechanic in Arlington Virginia where we settled and had our home and four children. He is buried there in Fairfax not far from where his family farm was, and I got that nice tombstone for his grave, because he was in the service for three years.

Raymond & Beverly on their wedding day September 1, 1949

Ed McCarthy: Navy USS Fargo, 1947

USS FARGO, LIGHT CRUISER

(From interviews June 2019 & June 2020)

Ed grew up in Norwalk Connecticut graduating Norwalk High in June 1947. He went to school with Stew Leonard who now has the World's Largest Dairy Store in town, and interesting in his school yearbook said, 'I want to be a millionaire!' The lesson there, be careful what you wish for, it just might come true!

Ed enlisted in the U.S. MARINES on July 10, 1947 a few weeks before his 18th birthday so his mother had to sign for him. A group of guys signed up for what was called the Connecticut Yankee Platoon, and headed down to Paris Island for boot camp aboard an old Pullman train.

They were attached to the USS Fargo a light cruiser out of New Port Rhode Island and spent two years making two trans-Atlantic trips to the Mediterranean Sea, one in 1948, and 1949. They were a part of the 6th fleet with a home port of Naples Italy, and also visited the city of Trieste on what was the Italian/Yugoslavian border and Nice France for Bastille day parade celebrations. The did practice maneuvers with amphibious landings on the Island of Malta, and Crete, and once back to the Americans, on Guantanamo Bay Cuba.

It was a time of peace and all was good. But just before leaving the service in July 9, 1950 the Korean War had broken out on June 25 of that same year.

Ed was able to return home and worked for his uncle at Electrolux in Old Greenwich as a forklift driver, a job he loved. But wanting to earn a trade and take advantage of the GI bill, like many returning veterans, he started night school at the old Center Junior High on School street in Norwalk attending the Union school for Plumbing.

He had grown up in South Norwalk with my mom Annie. One night at Phil Bakers restaurant, a popular local hangout, Ed was out with a buddy and ran into Annie and her girlfriend Helen. Some sparks started to fly and later at a family party at my uncle Tony Nardella's house, Helen and Ed started going steady and eventually married in June of 1954.

Ed was also our family plumber for many years along with his son Brian, and I also worked in banking with his daughter Anne Marie during my college days going back to 1979. At this writing they are both around 90 years of age married 66 years and are packing up the old house and getting ready to move to Florida. We wish them all the best!

A beautiful photo of USS Fargo in Venice Italy, en route to Trieste.

Bill Cabral: Air Force, Turkey, 1962

Rank: Airman First Class
Heavy Ground Radar Maintenance & Instructor

While stationed at Incirlik AFB Turkey, we worked on the Long Range Radar site that was monitoring our U2 spy plane, piloted then by Francis Gary Powers, when he was shot down over Russia. Our base went into immediate lock down! It turned out all communications from home newspapers had more information about our base than I even knew!

Dave VanBuskirk: Army, 1970

DATE ENLISTED:

U.S. Army Reserve, 1970 – Unit 344th Military Police; Hamden, CT.

BRANCH OF SERVICE: U.S. ARMY

BASIC TRAINING: Fort Jackson – Columbia, South Carolina. AIT (Advanced Training) Fort Gordon in Augusta, Georgia.

IN HIS WORDS:

I trained as Military Policeman, if activated would be sent to Vietnam for riverboat patrol. Overall, a six-year obligation. Note: Never activated – obligation – monthly meetings in Hamden, Conn. And active duties for two weeks each summer until end of 1976.

Saved fellow soldier during grenade training in South Carolina. A grenade was dropped and acting quickly I picked it up and threw it as far as possible away from the area. After completing my obligation in 1976 without ever being activated to go to Vietnam I considered myself very lucky! I served only in U.S. and night patrol in Georgia was a most interesting experience.

YOUR VIEW OF GOD & FAITH IN THE MIDST OF WAR & BATTLE:

It was conflicted – I was trained to kill and use a M – 16 rifle and a 45-caliber pistol. To this day I was never sure if I could actually kill someone. At the end of my obligation I remembered thinking life is too short, do not waste time. I was married and we started a family right after the military obligation was complete. I was always in banking before and during my Army Reserve obligation. My major conflict was the supreme belief in God vs. using my training to kill people. Luckily, I never saw combat. I always wondered if I could kill an enemy soldier! Each and every night during any military event I was involved in, prayer was my most important moment.

HOW YOU WERE CHANGED BY YOUR EXPERIENCE?

The fact that I had to use weapons that could kill people, often kept me up at night while on active duty.

KP Duty, getting to know and respect my Drill Sergeant (A man from Alabama). I believe the present generation would be well served to be asked to give some form of service to their country. Patriotism needs to make a comeback!

YOUR VIEW ON THIS PRESENT GENERATION & OUR COUNTRY'S DIRECTION:

My view on the present generation and the direction of our country is conflicted. I believe all U.S. Citizens should be required (if able) to serve in the military. When I served, we were a unit of 50% Black soldiers and 50% White, and we all got along, and joked around like friends and even brothers. Sadly we seem to be missing that today.

ANY OTHER ADDITIONAL THOUGHTS: The biggest conflict during my active duty was worrying about my wife, how she would cope if I was killed. Thank God I made it home alive.

Michael Nardella: Army National Guard, 1966

(Written in his words)

After High school in 1966 I enrolled in ROTC (Reserves Officers' Training Corps) at Providence College, Rhode Island. I studied military science for 4 years taught by professors who were army personal. This was followed by Infantry basic training in 1968 and active duty at the height of the Vietnam War and just prior to the Tet offensive. We were stationed at Indian Town Gap Reservation in Pennsylvania, (IGMR), an active military post, which would later after the war take in Vietnam refugees, many who came to be known as 'The Boat People' who fled in the wake of the incoming communist regime.

In 1970 I was commissioned as a second lieutenant, and reported to Fort Sill, Oklahoma for FAOBC (Field Artillery Officers Basic Course). At the time we were waiting on orders for Vietnam.

As it turned out the Army began to implement what was known as RIF (Reduction In Forces), and no longer needed officers since by 1971 the Vietnam conflict, or at least America's involvement, since Richard Nixon had been elected President, began winding down. So, I transitioned into Army National Guard in my home State of Connecticut.

My first assignment was with the 2nd battalion, 192 Field Artillery at the old armory in downtown Stamford. The following year a new armory was completed in my hometown of Norwalk in 1972. I spent the following six or seven years at various duties, promoted in 1973 to First Lieutenant assigned C -Battery as a fire direction officer. The Battery was equivalent to the Army's Infantry Company.

In 1976 my military obligation was over, but my commander wanted me to stay on to be Battery Commander. So, I reenlisted and by the mid-1980's I was promoted to Major. Again, taking on various staff duties, I was able to rise in the ranks to second in command as Battalion Executive Officer. In 1988 I was promoted to State Area Command STARC headquarters in Hartford.

As part of our active duty we had what was known as Civil Disturbance Training, basically for domestic problems that could arise here at home. We were called upon to provide added security during the 1982 Black Panther trial of Bobby Seale in New Haven. Then in 1983 after the Mianus River Bridge collapse we assisted police in Greenwich with traffic coordination. We would also continue doing a two-week stint for a what we called our once a drill a year, as most of us maintained a job back home outside of the Guard.

In light of the social protest and unrest taking place in our country at this time (June 2020) I would like to offer my view in the present political debate of expecting the President or Governors to call up the National Guard in time of crisis. Let us be clear, 99% of our training is of a military nature, meaning for combat. And historically as occurred at Kent State University in Ohio in 1970 when the guard was called upon to quell Vietnam protesters and restore order, bad things can happen. (Four students were killed). We are not comfortable with that roll as domestic policeman. That is something that people and politicians should take into consideration and weigh heavily before committing troops.

Later on, I took refresher courses again at Fort Sill, OK and Ft Drum NY and Camp Edwards, formerly known as Otis Air Force base, on Cape Cod. The reason for these trips was as an artillery officer my home state of Connecticut had no live fire range for training purposes. We also headed south for training in Virginia at Camp Pickett, interestingly, named for the Confederate general who led what proved the final fatal charge at Gettysburg, which then became a turning point in the Civil War.

The 192 Field artillery battery (Though deactivated now as of 2010) was the longest continuous serving active field artillery unit in the US Army! Our history battle streamers date back to the Union Army during the Civil War. We are awarded these streamers, which commemorate battle engagements, and post them on our flag colors. Our Motto was SKILL and FORCE. Our main weapon was the 105 mm Howitzer canon (See photo below). It saw a lot of use during WWII in both the European and Pacific theater as well as in Vietnam where it was fired from a platform.

I finished my duties in the National Guard in 1990 completing 24 years of total service and retired as a Major. I was proud to be the son of a WWII veteran, and proud to have served with my fellow troops in the preparedness and defense of our great country the good old USA!

PHOTOS: by Mike Nardella (used with permission) Some photos of Arms & equipment we used.

The first is a WWII vintage 105 mm M101A1 towed howitzer. It was used heavily in both Europe and during the Pacific island's invasions. This gun in a camouflaged firing position, live firing. The weapon is an indirect fire weapon. It employs a forward observer, who spots targets and relays data to the fire direction center. The FDC then converts this to firing commands and forwards it to the guns. This is the 101 being towed by its prime mover the 2 1/2 ton truck, the "deuce and a half". An Abrams tank on maneuvers. I spent most of my military career around this type of excellent field artillery weapons. Here we are doing strategic maneuvers planning.

NEW CENTURY: Pat Fern, Navy, WAR in IRAQ

THIS LAST STORY COVERS THE END OF THE 20th CENTURY AND THE NEW TYPE OF WARS THE UNITED STATES FACES.

It will also serve an introduction to our next volume:

'WAR STORIES OF THE 20th & 21st CENTURY: AFTER THE COLD WAR"

PATRICK FERN: THE GULF WAR

I have been in the military for almost 23 years now. The first 4 years I was on full active duty with the Navy. The last 18+ I have been in the Air Force reserves. While in the Air Force I have been overseas to Germany and worked in support of operations Iraqi Freedom and Enduring Freedom.

But it was really when I was in the Navy that I saw action. My squadron was attached to a Nimitz class carrier the USS Carl Vinson CVN 70. In October of 1998 until March of 1999, we were deployed to the Persian Gulf. This was for operations Desert Fox and Southern Watch. Since Congress didn't officially end the Gulf War until 2000, I was there for pretty much the tail end of the war. Let me just say we were very busy, without going into too many details. Not sure what may be classified or not still. But I was involved in several air-strikes launched against the Iraqi regime. It was very intense night after night.

Sincerely,
Patrick Fern
former AD3 US Navy and
Currently TSGT US Air Force.

MAPS: Europe & Pacific Theaters of War

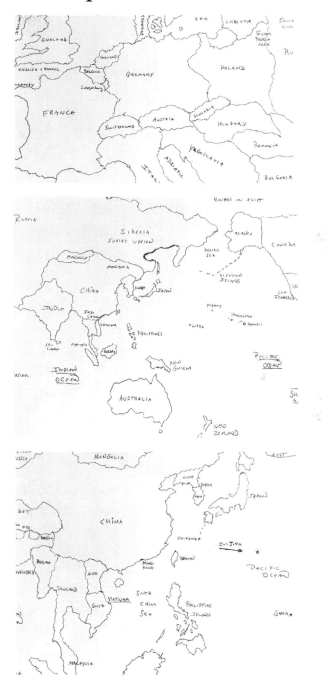

ORIGINS OF WAR: by Luke Cardamone

(Used with permission.)

The Paris Peace Conference began on January 18, 1919, the forty-eight-year anniversary of the proclamation of the German Empire. There were several peace treaties that were ratified in the months after World War One, however the Treaty of Versailles was the most significant treaty to arise from the aftermath of what was called, The Great War. Signed six months after the armistice of November 11, 1918 which ended the fighting across the war fronts, the Treaty of Versailles was eventually signed by Germany on June 28, 1919. Even though Germany did not agree with the harsh conditions they were charged with, they reluctantly signed the treaty since they were in no condition to dispute the ramifications. Therefore, the signing of the Versailles Treaty officially brought an end to the Great War between Germany and the Allied Powers. Wilson's Fourteen Points set the framework for the peace treaty which then created the foundation for foreign policy during what would later be known as the "inter-war period." German delegates were not present at any of the peace talk negotiations because Britain and France prevented them from participating since Germany had lost the war.

The Big Four debated one another at the peace conference continuously for months until common ground could eventually be agreed upon. The "Big Four" was comprised of France's Prime Minister Georges Clemenceau, Italy's Vittorio Emanuele Orlando, England's David Lloyd George and President Woodrow Wilson of the United States. However, Orlando eventually left the conference because his interests in the Adriatic and Mediterranean had been ignored by the other big three. These men were the important figures who were primarily responsible for the final outcome of the negotiation process. Determining how to appropriately reprimand Germany for the losses suffered in Europe was not an easy process. The redistribution of European empires and proper punishment of Germany proved to be a cumbersome challenge as Wilson often had greatly opposing views from Clemenceau and George. Each delegate proposed different types of ideas and regulations that would best address their respective countries' needs.

Germany was the primary target of the Treaty of Versailles, largely in part because they were held responsible for all the carnage caused during the war and did not have any delegates present at the peace conferences to defend themselves. The consequences bestowed upon them were seemingly impossible to fulfill since Germany did not have enough resources to fully payback their debts. The most controversial component of the Versailles Treaty was Article 231, best known as the "War Guilt clause" which demanded that Germany agree to several penalties such as decreasing their military, as well as to relinquish a great sum of money and colonial territories to mostly France and England. In reality, Germany simply did not have enough funds to reimburse all the demands that the Allied powers had requested, and the Allies were fully aware of this concern. As one could imagine, the severe punishments placed on Germany lead to an economic collapse in Germany, leaving the nation utterly depleted. Desperate for any kind of change that could help improve living conditions and bring back a resurgence of power to the state, Germany desperately sought a savior that would pull them from the ruins. The vulnerability of the German state allowed for a man named Adolf Hitler to rise to power who would then alter world history for decades.

Fourteen Points Woodrow Wilson was the first president of the United States to spend a significant amount of time overseas. He temporarily neglected his responsibilities in the United States and tried to negotiate with European delegates himself which ended up hurting his reputation with Congress. Wilson's points were very idealistic and could not fully be achieved as he had envisioned. Even though Wilson's Fourteen Points proved to be too idealistic to accomplish, they served the purpose of setting the framework for the Versailles Treaty which was negotiated in the Paris Peace Conference. When President Woodrow Wilson arrived in Europe following the conclusion of the war, he sought to bring peace and democracy to a broken Europe that had just endured the horrors of The First World War. Wilson was greeted by the French people with tremendous praise and was viewed as a hero. He planned to accomplish such relations with his Fourteen Points, or 'commandments' as Clemenceau sarcastically referred to them as with prepositions of peace and democracy on a global level in an attempt to prevent the emergence of another world conflict. An emphasis of free trade on a global scale, free navigation of the seas, elimination of empires and secret treaties as well as the de-colonization of Europe were all key components of Wilson's Fourteen Points designed to create a democratic future in Europe. Clemenceau exclaimed in frustration of Wilson, "He exasperates me with his four-teen commandments when the good God had only ten." – Peace Set-tlements, pg 6. The French and English Empires were not particularly fond of the proposed banishment of secret treaties and the national self-determination of colonies as it jeopardized their influence around the globe.

While Wilson believed that Germany must repay the Allies for the war damages they caused, he did not want to punish Germa-ny too harshly in fear that Germany's economy may collapse and bring down with it the rest of Europe. However, Clemenceau (and George to an extent) were less forgiving than Wilson and wanted to implement harsher punishments against Germany. On the night of November 11, 1918 after the armistice went into effect, Clemenceau famously stated, "We have won the war: now we have to win the peace, and that may be more difficult" – Peace Settlements. After all, the war was fought on the battlegrounds of Europe and not the Unit-ed States, so countries such as France in particular had suffered some of the greatest casualties to both their population and landscape. "The Fourteen Points were too imprecise to constitute the basis for a peace treaty. Wilson had not set forth a rigorous guide for action and few of the points made definite statements. The resulting vagueness of the Fourteen Points ruled out the possibility of it ever serving as a con-tract, however the lack of precision is what allowed the points to be negotiated and accepted by the Allies" Armistice 1918, page 27.

The first point Wilson made stated that there were to be no more secret treaties, Wilson felt these were responsible for creating territori-al disputes during World War One, especially in the Ottoman Empire.

The Ottomans had been on a steady decline since the mid nineteenth century and it was apparent to the world that its collapse was inevitable. Once England had entered Constantinople, they began to propose complex secret treaties that contradicted one another. To make matters worse, Wilson wanted nothing to do with the secret treaties because he believed they were undemocratic and opposed the ideals of his Fourteen Points. "Wilson's second point which emphasized 'freedom of the seas' became one of his most controversial points. It was meant to give absolute protection to Maritime rights of neutral nations but failed to specify the exact details. The third point was intended to remove all economic barriers in Europe while the fourth point focused on the disarmament of European nations. Wilson's fifth point, 'absolutely impartial adjustments of all colonial claims' was intended to nullify the treaties that the Allies secretly made before the US entered the war in 1917" - Armistice 1918, page 27. President Wilson emphasized the importance of returning 'stolen' territories back to their respective countries and redefining such countries borders based on what language people of the area spoke. Wilson's sixth point addressed the newly established Soviet Union which was a communist regime lead by Vladimir Lenin. Being a strong advocate of democracy, Wilson feared that Lenin's influence if left unchecked may spread across the rest of Europe and corrupt the governments that Wilson was desperately trying to make democratic. This point in short called for an evacuation of all Russian territory to secure the best and freest cooperation of the other nations of the world so that new national policies may welcome the emergence of free nations. In his seventh point, Wilson wanted Belgium to be evacuated as well and its sovereignty restored. The eight point was well received by Clemenceau since it called for the restoration of all invaded portions of France, in particular the Alsace-Lorraine territory was to be returned to the French.

One of the largest battles to occur during The Great War was the Gallipoli Campaign which was a large-scale amphibious assault by the Allies on Constantinople in an attempt to gain control of the Dardanelle Straits. The campaign raged on for months as a series of bloody battles lead to a large number of casualties suffered for both the Ottomans and the British/Australian forces. Eventually, British forces were forced to retreat after landing on the beaches of Constantinople and suffered a harsh blow to their navy and ground forces. The outcome of the campaign was considered to be the last major victory of the Ottoman Empire before it collapsed during the inter-war period. Wilson's twelfth point assured the Ottomans some sovereignty in Constantinople, however other nationalities under Turkish control were now given the opportunity to seek their own independence. In addition, the Dardanelle Straits were to be permanently opened as a free passage to the ships and commerce of all nations under international guarantees.

Point thirteen sought to resurrect Poland as an independent state with free and secure access to the seas as well as regaining European territories that contained indisputable Polish populations. This was another point that France strongly agreed with because strengthening the 'new' Polish state came at Germany's expense. Clemenceau believed that a strong Polish state to Germany's east and a strong French sate to Germany's west would be enough to contain and control any future German aggression.

League of Nations Wilson's fourteenth and final point called for a general association of nations. There was little to no controversy over this point as most of the Allies had already unofficially formed the League of Nations. One of the biggest flaws of the Peace Conference negotiation was that German delegates were not permitted entry nor were they allowed to join the League of Nations. Regardless of some controversial points that were heavily debated, President Wilson's Fourteen Points were accepted by the Allies and his 'Wilsonian program' made an honest effort to eliminate the threat of a potential war. However, it was the intentional use of broad terminology throughout the document that both allowed for the Allied Powers to agree on peace terms but also for countries to develop different understandings than what Wilson had implied. The creation of the League of Nations was ultimately designed to prevent another world war, but the United States Senate did not agree with the League of Nations

and feared it would deprive Congress the constitutional right to declare war as well as be dragged into a future world conflict that may
be irrelevant to their own concerns. The United States Congress did
not sign the treaty of Versailles even though President Wilson helped
create the conditions of the treaty for months in Paris. Finally, in July
1921, the American government declared a joint resolution for peace
ending the state of war with Germany. The United States then entered
an isolationist policy as did England out of fear that they would be
drawn into war along with the United States. This left France alone
attempting to run the League of Nations with little help which did
not go well.

By November of 1918, the monarchs who had controlled the Central Powers (Germany, Austro-Hungarian and Bulgaria) had all fled
their respective countries and went into exile. This allowed for new
political regimes to emerge in their absence. Italy became the first fas-
cist regime in Europe under the dictation of Benito Mussolini. Adolf
Hitler (a former German soldier in World War One) then created the
Nazi Party which rose to power in Germany during the late 1920's
and early 1930's. After the Czar in Russia is murdered and the country breaks out into a civil war, Vladimir Lenin lead Russia to become
a communist nation called the Soviet Union. Many countries across
Europe undergo political revolutions after the war while democracy
begins to be pushed aside for opposing political regimes. The fact that
the United States did not join the League of Nations to help regulate
as it had planned lead to its inevitable downfall. The French then prepared for the next war by investing billions of dollars into a defensive
front between France and Germany known as the Maginot Line. It
was comprised of a system of concrete bunkers with heavy artillery,
machine gun nests and underground tunnels equipped with barracks
and radio stations. When World War Two does break out, the Nazis
implement their blitzkrieg tactics to storm the western front which
only takes the Nazis two days to breach Maginot line with paratroopers and panzer tanks.

War Guilt clause Article 231 of the Versailles Treaty also known
as the "War Guilt clause" listed the bitter reparations that Germany

was expected to fully pay back to the Allies with cash, natural resources and territories. Germany was held entirely responsible for
war even though a Serbian nationalist had 'sparked the fuse' that
dragged Europe into the war and the Russians were the first military to ready their troops for combat. The treaty deeply humiliated
the German people, especially future generations who did not fight
in the war but were still expected to continue the repayments. Germany was forced to economically reimburse the Allies by virtually
singing a blank check. France, Britain and the United States were well
aware that Germany did not nearly have enough money to pay back
the large war debt, however they proceeded with the harsh war guilt
punishments regardless of potential consequences. The War Guilt
clause addressed three main types of reparations: military, territorial
and economic.

Military: The War Guilt clause stated that Germany would not
be allowed to maintain an air force, the use of poison gas, heavy artillery or submarine warfare, all which played a prominent role in
Germany's military tactics during the First World War. Their navy
would be restricted to only six battleships with an inadequate number of smaller warships. Furthermore, the German army was limited
to a maximum capacity of only 100,000 men with a tight restraint on
the number of rifles, machine guns, ammunition and production of
other military goods, which were to be supervised by the Allies. All
German fortifications along the western front were obligated to be
neutralized to reassure peaceful relations with France by maintaining a buffer between France and Germany. To further strengthen the
buffer, Clemenceau pushed for the Rhineland to be de-militarized to
secure the area along the French-German border. "The military pro-
visions of the Versailles Treaty graphically underlined the Allied de-
termination to safeguard their own future security against German
aggression. The German Army was reduced to 100,000 men and the
Navy to 15,000. Conscription was forbidden to prevent the training
of more men and the period of service for the new Regular Army was
to be limited to twelve years for men, and twenty-five for officers"
– Germany 1919-1939, page 15. In addition to their military being re-

duced to a bare minimum, Germany was not allowed to unite with their former allies from the Great War.

After World War One, several countries emerged from the ruins of former empires and gained their independence for the first time. The Austro-Hungarian Empire was one of Germany's largest allies during the war but, collapsed after their defeat and was broken into several different countries: Czechoslovakia, Yugoslavia, Bosnia, Serbia, Croatia and Slovenia. Even though Austria was predominantly a German speaking country, they were separated from Germany and were forbidden to merge with one another. By May of 1919, the Allies had presented the Versailles Treaty to German delegates and to little surprise, Germany was outraged by the treaty's conditions. German delegates desperately wanted to negotiate the treaty, but the Big Four would not tolerate any form of compromise. The Allied forces made it clear that if German delegates did not sign and accept the conditions of the treaty, then military forces would resume their attack on Germany. Citizens were rioting in the streets and the German military was in no shape to further defend themselves against an Allied advancement. With their hands tied and their backs against the wall, German delegates reluctantly signed the treaty on June 28, the fifth anniversary of the assassination of the Archduke Franz Ferdinand. The treaty was signed in the Hall of Mirrors of the Versailles Palace just outside of Paris where German officials had proclaimed the German Empire back in 1871. John Maynard Keynes, a world-renowned British economist of the early 20th century disagreed strongly with the terms of the "peace negotiations" and resigned from his position as Treasurer. In late 1919, Keynes published, "The Economic Consequences of Peace" which articulated his criticisms of the war reparation clauses and predicted the long term economic and political instability that would plague all of Europe as a result.

Territorial: Deciding how to appropriately handle the territories of collapsed empires and emerging countries during the Paris Peace conference was one of the most tedious tasks to accomplish. Clemenceau had the most ambitious agenda of the Big Four and planned to expand France's borders at Germany's expense. As a result of the negotiation process, the Alsace-Lorraine territory was restored back under French control after Germany had previously taken control of the region in 1871. In addition to Alsace-Lorraine, France wanted to annex several more of German territories to expand their power in Western Europe, however England was hesitant to proceed with these ideas as they feared it may jeopardize the status of their own empire. The British Empire had been the most dominant empire in Western Europe for centuries prior to the war and with France having a long running rivalry with Britain, George was not too eager to agree with all of Clemenceau's bold prepositions. Clemenceau made a case for annexing the Rhineland to "complete" France's natural border and fortify the safety net between France and Germany, but George did not want to tip the balance of power and Wilson believed the annexation would contradict his Fourteen Points. "The German territories west of the Rhine, together with the bridgeheads of Mainz, Coblenz and Cologne were to be occupied by Allied troops. The demilitarization of the west bank of the Rhine was enforced, together with a 50-kilometer-wide strip on the east bank of the river. Finally, the French received a guarantee of military support from America and Britain in the event of a potential attack by Germany, which concluded on the same day of the Versailles Treaty." –Germany 1919-1939, page 16. In an attempt to satisfy each delegate, the Big Four agreed on a compromise that required Germany to demilitarize the Rhineland so that their military forces would not infringe upon the neutral zone between France and Germany.

The French continued to fortify their defenses with a large investment in the Maginot Line as mentioned earlier. During the late 1920's and into the 1930's, Hitler had seemingly played by the rules of the Versailles Peace treaty when in reality he was secretly preparing his troops for another World War. In 1934, Hitler signed the Non-Aggression Pact between Germany and Poland 'guarantying' peaceful relations between the two countries. A year later in 1935, Hitler officially renounced the Versailles Treaty and continued to test his luck with the Allies. By 1936 Hitler was nearly ready to declare war and had remilitarized the Rhineland, Britain and the United States remained unresponsive and did not intervene. France feared the next war was dangerously close and was dependent on Britain and the United States to rush to their defense in the case of German aggression.

The Saar territory in Germany provided the country with a great source of coal which was used to fuel Germany's infrastructure. Continuing to pursue his bold ambitions, Clemenceau wanted to claim the Saar territory for France as another form of repayment but George and Wilson prevented this from happening. Instead, the Saar coal mines were to be turned over to the League of Nations for the next fifteen years and then after that time its inhabitants were allowed to return to German rule if they wanted to do so which they ended up doing in 1935. Wilson, Clemenceau and George continued to debate how they were going to deal with Germany's borders and the emergence of new countries, especially in Eastern Europe. Denmark remained neutral during the war and wanted to stay clear from any aggression in the inter-war period. As a result, North Schleswig was then returned to the Danish after it was lost in 1864 while southern Schleswig remained a German territory. Denmark feared that if they reacquired the entire Schleswig territory then it would lead to hostility between them and Hitler in the near future.

The re-emergence of Poland (illustrated in the Fourteen Points) as a sovereign state proved to be another difficult task for the Big Four to handle. Territorial redistribution continued to diminish the East German empire when Poland, who had just re-emerged as a sovereign country was then carved out of the German Empire by giving a great deal of German farmland over to the Polish. "It was in East Europe that Germans felt most ill-treated. To give the new Polish state the access to the sea which Wilson's points had demanded, the Polish Corridor was created—the provinces of Posen and West Prussia being lost to Poland. Apart from the damage to Germany's national pride of Poland's victory, there was the fact that Poland along with the other small states in East Europe, became the center of France's policies in East Europe." – Germany 1919-1939, page 16-17. "Poland, which had ceased to exist as a sovereign state in the eighteenth century while it was divided among Russia, Prussia and Austria now re-emerged in the wake of the collapse of those empires; but defining the re-born Poland's frontiers would pose a serious problem." – Peace Settlements, pg. 2. The new Polish government wanted to claim even more German territories that would further expand the size of the original Polish state. France supported a large and powerful Polish state because it could then act as another European power to keep Germany "in check" due to its border with Germany opposite of France. In correlation with point two of the Fourteen Points, Wilson supported Polish access to the sea to prevent them from being a land locked country. This led to Poland acquiring the German port city of Danzig as well as most of West Prussia, the districts of Ellenstein and Marie Werder and upper Silesia. The Danzig port was arguably the most important territory Poland had acquired because it provided them with direct access to the Vistula River which ran along a narrow strip of land called the "Polish Corridor" that connected Poland to the Baltic Sea. The new additions to the Polish state both geographically separated East Prussia from Germany and gave Poland access to the sea which Germany believed they were supposed to receive. Needless to say, the results of the Peace Conference delegations further agitated the German people and provoked Hitler to eventually invade Poland in September 1939 to regain lost territory. Hitler's invasion of Poland marked the official outbreak of World War Two which proved to be a premature decision on Hitler's part. In the same year, Hitler signed a Non-Aggression Pact with the Soviet Union but, quickly disregarded it when he invaded the Soviets two years later in the summer of 1941.

The German Empire did not have as many colonial territories as France or England's however, they did have a few colonies in mostly Africa, the Pacific and some in Asia. "Both before and during World War One, The British and German Empire's respectively had significantly positioned colonies in Africa and Asia. Even though the British Empire was larger than Germany's, the British felt that German colonies in central and southern Africa particularly created a potential threat to the British Empire. The debate for control over the route to India, Egypt and southern Africa was a huge struggle during the short years prior to the Paris Peace Conference." – Britain & Germany's Lost Colonies 1914-1919, page 16. During the war, France and Britain held secret treaties which discussed the distribution of Germany's colonies overseas. The European Allies feared that Germany's colonies were a threat to their own respective empires and felt it was mandatory for them to redistribute the German colonies. President Wilson wanted to maintain democratic ideals that would attempt to promote self-determination in Germany's colonies. In an attempt to leave behind imperialistic views of the past, the German colonies ended up being controlled by the League of Nations so that they could monitor each territory. "Under this arrangement Britain received control of German East Africa (Tanganyika); Belgium took control of Ruanda-Urundi (Rwanda and Burundi); Britain and France divided the Cameroons and Togoland, with the bulk going to France; South Africa received South-West Africa (Namibia); most of the German Pacific islands south of the equator were assigned to Australia, except German Samoa and Nauru which went to New Zealand; and the islands north of the equator went to Japan" – Peace Settlement, pg. 14. The War Guilt clause continued to dismantle the German Empire by reducing their military capacity and tearing down the country's borders. These limitations were not enough to fulfill Germany's war debt as the Big Four still needed to decide how much money Germany would have to pay in reparations.

Economic: The economic war reparations demanded of Germany in the War Guilt clause were arguably the grimmest conditions of all that really rubbed the salt in Germany's fresh wounds. The German people were expected to fully repay the Allies for the losses of non-military property as well as a "penalty fee" for waging war and then being defeated. War is an extremely expensive investment for every country that gets involved as it requires a great sum of government spending on equipment such as vehicles, weapons, and ammunition. Not to mention the vast number of brave men and women who ultimately sacrifice their lives to serve their country. President Wilson of the United States was the only delegate who was not in favor of placing an indemnity on Germany that would burden them with a massive war debt for decades. France and Britain respectively wanted to squeeze every penny that they could out of the Germans, but Wilson opposed because he knew that Germany would never be able to fully pay back such severe reparations. As a result, the German economy would collapse while potentially bringing down the rest of Europe with it. However, George and Clemenceau convinced Wilson that the non-military reparations should include war pensions which essentially doubled the amount of money that Germany would owe the Allies.

By March of 1919, it became clear that the French still wanted to annex the Rhineland as well as the fact that Britain understood that Germany could not be economically crippled and still be expected to fully repay their war debts. "The German central bank, the Reichsbank, held gold reserves of only 2.4 billion gold marks, far below any estimate of what the reparations bill would reach. Germany could, potentially, pay in the form of manufactured goods or labor to assist in reconstruction. The Allies held divided views on these possibilities as well. It was clear that the powerful trade unions in Belgium and France would not accept free labor payments, while Britain had no desire to see German goods taking its markets; determining a final sum seemed impossible" Peace settlements, pg. 17. Later in June, when Germany was forced to sign the treaty, they signed a blank check which would allow the Allies to decide on any amount of money they felt necessary to complete the reparations. By August of 1919, the German government was bestowed twenty billion gold marks of debt and was expected to begin making routine payments. On top of that, Germany was obligated to provide the League of Nations with thirty-eight million tons of coal per year for the next ten years. The reparations due to be collected ultimately destroyed Germany as Wilson and the British economist Keynes had feared. The German economy collapsed almost instantaneously and by the 1920's the degree of inflation was so extreme that German currency had essentially lost all its value. The government attempted to repay the Allies by printing a magnificent sum of money, but this only made matters worse by driving the value of currency further into the ground. In fact, grocery shopping required a wheel barrel full of money stacks which even then was barely enough to purchase a few simple items.

No country wants to find themselves on the losing side of a costly war as Germany did in 1918. The Allied and Central Powers exhausted their resources and population in an expensive war that raged on for four long years. After the armistice was signed, the Allies got to work to decide the fate of Germany who was to be held responsible for the war damages. I maintain that excluding German delegates out of the peace conference negotiations and League of Nations ended up becoming the biggest blunder during the inter-war period. Even though Germany had been defeated, they should have been allowed a presence of delegates at the conference to prevent the Big Four from drafting the War Guilt clause which further destroyed Germany and humiliated its people. A German presence would have likely led to a more reasonably balanced outcome of the treaty and not urged Germany to seek revenge twenty years later. Of course everything is presented more clearly in hindsight, but I cannot help but think that if there had been a presence of German delegates to counter the unnecessarily harsh negotiations, then the Second World War most likely could have been averted and Europe could have enjoyed a democratic future as American President Wilson had envisioned.

Bibliography

Gathorne-Hardy, Geoffrey. *The Fourteen Points and the Treaty of Versailles.* New York: Farrar and Rinehart Inc, 1939.

Goldstein, Erik. *The First World War Peace Settlements 1919-1925.* London: Pearson Education, 2002.

Hacken, Richard and Plotke, Jane. "The Peace Treaty of Versailles." Brigham Young University, Accessed March 18, 2019.

Henig, Ruth. *Versailles and After, 1919-1933.* London, New York: Routledge: 1995.

Hiden, John. *Germany and Europe 1919-1939.* London & New York: Longman Group Limited, 1977.

Hillgruber, Andreas. *Germany and the Two World Wars.* Cambridge, Massachusetts and London, England: Harvard University

Press, 1981.

Louis, William Roger. *Great Britain and Germany's Lost Colonies.* London: Oxford University Press, 1967.

Lowry, Bullitt. *Armistice 1918.* Kent, Ohio and London, England: The Kent State University Press, 1996.

Luckau, Alma. *The German Delegation at the Paris Peace Conference.* New York: Columbia University Press, 1941 (reprint 1971).

Magana, Carlos. "Signing of the Versailles Treaty." University of California, Santa Barbara, Accessed March 18, 2019.

Marston, Frank Swain. *The Peace Conference of 1919: Organization and Procedure.* Westport, Connecticut: Greenwood Press Publishers, 1944 (reprint 1981).

POEMS

Poem: submitted by Mike Kardos from his parents in WWII February 10, 2020

NAME: KARDOS

John, this is a letter poem, my mother wrote to my father during WWII. He was a flight engineer on a B-29 in China, Burma, India theatre. I hope this helps. You can borrow it for your book. Mike Kardos.

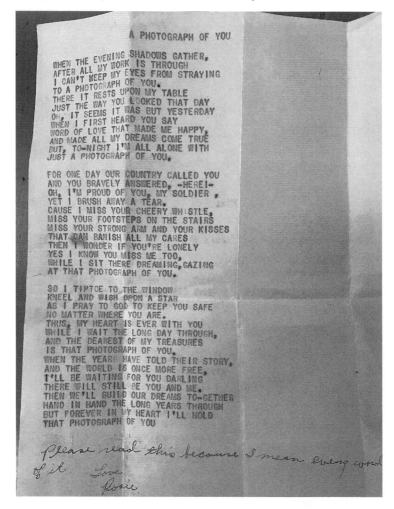

Farewell My Soldier Friend: Rev. J.P.C.

Written by Pastor John Cardamone
Georgetown Bible Church September 2000

"I awoke this morning to hear the church bell toll,
And remembered not to ask for Whom…
I bid you Farewell my Soldier Friend.
Your final battle has come to an end.
May you now rest from your weary life
The many battles of pain and strife
I trust you knew the One who died for you
And the Hope of Christ is yours now true

You fought so valiantly at a time when tyranny did rule
And stood against the tide of evil, and purchased freedom for not
a few
Do we remember what is was like?
When wrong was ruled by the dark gun of might?
And all the world seemed lost in hopeless night…

But then a glimmer, a ray of hope
As God gave us men who knew the cost
Of freedom in our way of life that was purchased by those who
had gone before
And faced the darkness of deaths door
That we might know the light of Life
And freedom from tyranny, and strife.

But most of all we must remember Him
Who did purchase the truest of Liberty
Upon the Old Rugged Cross of Calvary
To save All sinners, even a wretch like me
Tis Amazing Grace the sweetest sound
That we might see that eternal day
And know lasting freedom forever stay

So, I bid you farewell my soldier friend
God speed, and I trust we shall meet again
In the land where no tears do ever fall
And God brings peace to one and all
Who call upon His Holy name and eternally with Him shall reign
And receive forgiveness in Jesus, The Same

We'll wait till He fights the last battle of death
And brings all sorrow and pain to it's final end
Until then, I bid you farewell, my soldier friend..."

Loving a soldier: Vietnam: Author Unknown

```
                    LOVING A SOLDIER

        LOVING A SOLDIER IS NOT AT ALL GAY
        FOR WITH YOUR HEART IS THE PRICE YOU MUST PAY
        IT'S BEING ALONE MOSTLY AND NOT TO HOLD
        BEING IN LOVE AND FEELING OLD.
        IT'S SENDING A LETTER WITH A STAMP UPSIDEDOWN
        TO A FAR AWAY LOVE IN A FAR AWAY TOWN.
        BEING IN LOVE WITH MOSTLY YOUR DREAMS
        BRING THOUGHTS OF HEAVEN WHERE LOVE'S LIGHT GLEAMS
        YOU WISH IT WERE POSSIBLE FOR HIM TO PHONE
        YOU WANT TO HEAR HIM SAY, "I'M ON MY WAY HOME."
        AND IF HE COMES IT'S LAUGHTER TOGETHER,
        UNCONSCIOUS OF PEOPLE, OF TIME AND OF WEATHER.
        IT'S WAVING GOOD-BYE TO A SOLDIER AT THE PHONE
        AND WONDERING WHEN YOU'LL SEE HIM AGAIN.
        AND RELUCTANLY, PAINFULLY TELLING HIM TO GO,
        AND INSIDE YOU ARE CRYING, WANTING HIM SO.
        YOU WAIT FOR MONTHS, NO WORDS FOR A SPELL
        AND WHEN YOU RECIEVE LETTERS, YOU BUBBLE WITH JOY
        AND ACT LIKE A KID WITH A NEW SHINNY TOY.
        LOVING A SOLDIER HAS UNTOLD FEARS
        CRYING UNTIL THERE ARE NO MORE TEARS.
        AND HATING THE WORLD, YOURSELF AND THE WAR,
        BECAUSE IT TOOK THE ONE YOU ADORE.
        GOING TO CHURCH TO KNEEL AND TO PRAY
        YOU KEEP LOVING HIM MORE EACH DAY
        YES, LOVING A SOLDIER IS BITTERNESS AND TEARS,
        IT'S LONELINESS, SADNESS AND UNFOUND FEARS.
        LOVING A SOLDIER IS REALLY NO FUN,
        BUT IT'S WORTH IT WHEN HIS DUTY IS DONE.


                        AUTHOR

                      UNKNOWN
```

Submitted by Dave Zavory from his late wife Joanne, during Vietnam 1968.

MONUMENTS & THE FLAG

At the time of this writing there is a significant and even often violent debate taking place in our nation over monuments and statues especially of War figures and what we call or once considered our national heroes. As a country we have a history of placing such remembrances in our communities all over the towns and cities of our great country, most especially the National monuments in our nation's Capital. I am including these photos of Civil War memorials I took when I lived in the DC area 30 years ago. They may soon be moved to some type of new Civil War memorial or museum or stored away altogether and hidden from public view. And though we may choose no longer to celebrate such monuments because of the pain associated with them for many Americans, we must not forget all that they represent which was part of our Nation's past.

We are coming to realize there is in a sense storm clouds that have passed over us as a nation that we certainly are not as homogeneous in our thinking as perhaps we had hoped, and that often these monuments and statues can represent different things to different people depending upon their background and their life experience. Perhaps we need a new type of museum that permits such reflection as a people.

And as such, these places I believe can mirror the intentions and three main goals of this book project as stated previously: First, to remember the history. It has been said that, with all its mistakes and painful lessons.

Second, to honor the sacrifices of those courageous and brave soldiers, men and women who in these noble causes, gave of themselves, that we might know liberty.

And third, to strive to prevent future wars. So that those lessons of pain and cost that such conflict inflicts upon a nation and its people, might be used in Lincoln's words *'to bind up those wounds.'*

Let us take a moment to remember and reflect, upon the lives of those who have secured our Liberty and the gift they granted to us, in our Freedom to debate such things, so that their story or sacrifice, and the millions of silenced voices shall never be forgotten.

Rev Johnny Cardamone, 5th of July 2020

SHEA MEMORIAL @ CALF PASTURE BEACH
NORWALK, CONNECTICUT:

"Come and Sit with Us and We Shall Speak of Freedom."

World War II:

'Soldier rest, the warfare over, dream of fighting fields no more.'

"McGrath WWII"

"They were Separated in Death by Time and Distance; They are Untied Here by Bravery and Honor."

KOREAN WAR:

"I did not know the dignity of their birth, but I do know the glory of their death."

General Douglas MacArthur

Tribute to Korean War Dead

"They played here as boys, They left us in their youth,
They served as men, They died as heroes,
They live again, Forever enshrined in the heart of this grateful City."

THE VIETNAM WAR PLAQUE:

"Greater love hath no man, than that he lay down his life for his friend." Gospel of St. John

"Dedicated to The Eternal Memory of These Brave Men From Norwalk, Who Gave Their Last Full Measure of Devotion, So That We Might Enjoy The Blessings of Everlasting Freedom."

Daniel Shea, Vietnam

GLOBAL WAR ON TERROR:

'Those who have long enjoyed such privileges as we enjoy forget in time that men have died to win them.' FDR.

FLAGS AT THE SHORE LINE:

Shea Memorial Flags Norwalk, Conn July 20, 2020

St John's Veterans cemetery, Norwalk, Connecticut

'Here they sleep in eternal rest from life's battles, these our sacred soldiers of liberty, awaiting the day of judgment and their final rest and reward; Remember them Always, for we shall join them soon.' Rev. J.P.C.

Our Beautiful American Flag: In spite of all, may God bless her and may she forever wave in Liberty!

My mother raised me to be a patriot! She too is buried at St. John's and I hope she would be proud of me for what has been this 25-year labor of love. Rev. J.P.C.

GEORGETOWN VFW RECOGNITION:

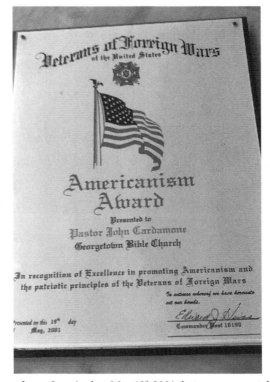

This was an honor I received on May 19ᵗʰ 2001 that means a great deal to me.

OLD FAMILY FLAG THAT HANGS IN MY HOME PRAYER CHAPEL

"I Pledge Allegiance to the Flag, of the United States of America, and to the Republic for which it stands, One Nation, Under God, Indivisible, with Liberty and Justice for All."

If our nation is to be strong and united, we must together believe and work for these words

It is under this banner, that so many of our brave patriots fought and died to preserve our Liberty.

WAR & PEACE-POLITICS & THE BIBLE

World Peace has been the elusive goal of humanity it would seem, since time began. The first war ever in history took place in the Garden of Eden. It was a war for the soul of mankind. The Holy Scripture tells us in Genesis 3, that The Evil One came in tempting disobedience to GOD'S only command at the time. And of course, the woman and the man ate of the tree of the knowledge of good and evil, and we have reaped the consequences for these last 6,000+ years. And then to add insult to injury the first man born becomes a murderer in Genesis 4 when Cain kills his brother Abel. He is confronted by God for the shedding of innocent blood, he replies with those immortal words, often taken out of context, "Am I My brother's Keeper?"

And so the Old Testament (OT) is the history of the Hebrew people from the call of Abraham in 2000 BC to the struggle and deliverance from slavery some 500 years later by the Prophet Moses. In Exodus 5:3 The Hebrew leaders request of Pharaoh to allow them to journey into the wilderness to Worship and offer sacrifice to the LORD our God lest He fall upon us with pestilence or with the sword. The people feared plague and war, always a sign that God had removed His blessing from them, and the nation.

This Biblical struggle continued in the conquest by Joshua of "The Promised Land" of Canaan, as war marked much of their ancient history. King David and his imprecatory Psalms were filled with a people's desire for vengeance against their enemies. (Psalm 5:8; Ps 13:4; Ps 23:5; Ps 143:3,12)

But as we transition to the New Testament dispensation, the words of the Rabbi and Messiah. Jesus of Nazareth in The Gospels strikes a different tone. In St. Matthew 5:9 of The Beatitudes Jesus declares, 'Blessed are the Peacemakers, for they shall be called sons of God' And in verse 44 to He instructs us to 'love your enemy' and pray for them. But Jesus also warned His disciples in Matthew 24:5 not to expect WORLD PEACE, in our lifetimes or until the End of time, because there would be 'Wars and rumors of War..."

Yet still there is something we clamor for deep in our soul and that of all people for every nation hold onto a desire for, peace and prosperity. Where does one hope to find then this 'KEY TO WORLD PEACE?' May we suggest beginning with The Shema of Deuteronomy 6, a book in the Old Testament Torah that Jesus quoted from more than any other. His sermon is found in St. Matthew chapter 22 The New Commandment:

'To love God will all our heart, soul, mind, and strength and to love our neighbor as ourselves.'

The prophets of the OT spoke of a time in the future when *'Swords would be beat into Plowshares."* (Isaiah 2:3 and Micah 3:4) I remember in 6th grade in 1970 visiting the United Nations in New York city and seeing this inscription written in stone. Still the world waits.

The seeds of war began when hatred, evil, envy and jealousy entered the human race in the Garden of Eden. It is a war within the souls of our first mother and father, Eve & Adam. The source of all future evil in this world is manifested and described as a Serpent who had entered the garden to beguile our ancient mother, and father, with the temptation to want something more than we have. Lust of the flesh, lust of the eyes, and boastful pride of life.

Wars also have begun due to the specter of revenge! WWI was triggered in 1914 with the assassination of the Archduke Ferdinand in Sarajevo and required justice. 'No Justice, No Peace' is a cry familiar in our own USA here in June of 2020! And of course, WWII begins for America the day after the infamous attack of our US naval base in Pearl Harbor.

Wars are started because people from one nation want something that people from another nation have and had no intention of sharing! WWII is a clear example as Hitler and the German Nazi party in Europe wanted the Sudetenland, and other territory. And in Asia and the Pacific the Japanese wanted more territory and natural resources, especially oil! The United States has in the past 40+ years had our own series of conflicts to ensure the flow of oil resources especially from the Middle East.

The late President Ronald Reagan was known to have liked to quote a favorite Russian proverb; *'Trust but Verify!'* This often-irked

Premier Gorbachev of the former Soviet Union. But in the end, they developed a trust and even friendship which helped bring about the end of The Cold War. The debate over the justification of the Iraq War in 2003 continues to this day. At a cost of over a trillion dollars, not to mention the thousands of lives lost as in every conflict both military and civilian, it raised the question of our ability to trust 'our intelligence assets' or for that matter our leaders! The third premise of this book is 'to prevent future war.' So, permit me to enter the debate a bit.

The argument at the time in 2002 was that supposedly Saddam still had WMD's (Weapons of Mass Destruction). This was the position of President George W. Bush, #43, V.P. Dick Cheney, Secretary of Defense Donald Rumsfeld, and his deputy Paul Wolfowitz, an early advocate and often referred to as the architect of the Iraq War (see Wikipedia).

Secretary of State General Colin Powell also was a key figure in the administration at the time. (EDITOR'S NOTE: I actually lived in Arlington Virginia in 1988 near Colin Powell and a contractor buddy of mine use to work on Volvos with him. I regret now I never had the time to join my friend and meet Powell! However, during this time I also worked as a house painter and did get to paint Lieutenant Colonel Oliver North's infamous fence! And I must say, he was a real Christian gentleman. We also had the same barber!)

Getting back to Iraq, I believe the Norwegian inspector from the UN spent nearly 6 months at the end of 2002 searching the Iraq countryside for WMD'S but found virtually nothing.

But the then Bush #43 administration seemed bent on war, some speculated to exact revenge for Saddams' assassination threat upon his father, President George Bush # 41. And so the drum beat to war continued, with most of the Senate voting at the time to support this resolution.

I recall around this same time watching a TV documentary I believe on 20/20 ABC one night, in which they interviewed Saddam Hussein girlfriend I believe. She said that his favorite singer was Frank Sinatra, his favorite song, 'Strangers in the Night' and his favorite movie, 'The Godfather'! Right there I knew at heart he sounded more like a bit of a hopeless romantic then a hard-brutal dictator, which no doubt he demonstrated he was. But my point there was perhaps in this information a bit of a window into his soul. And I predicted he would give up without firing a shot. Which of course he did when he was cornered and climbed out of that 'Spider Hole' on December 13, 2003, and he said, "Don't shoot! I am Saddam Hussein the president of Iraq!"

The point is we Must be able to have confidence in our leaders when they call a nation to war. This is the greatest sacred duty especially of a President as Commander in Chief to ask young men and women to risk their lives for our freedom. And so, I ask do we have political leaders we can trust? Is it possible in spite of All of our sophisticated intelligence that they may be blind and can't see the forest for the trees in 'The Great Swamp' of Washington DC? Of course, the alternative to blindness is deception, thinking the American people lack the ability or awareness to catch on! In a day of accusations of 'Fake News' this is the great duty of a free objective press under our constitution.

If our American system of government is to run with integrity and as such, to prevent mischief, it requires the participation of All of her citizens!

We are in the midst of a time of domestic division, unrest, protest, even rioting and some would fear revolution! In words most often attributed to Ben Franklin,

'WE MUST EITHER ALL HANG TOGETHER OR WE SHALL ALL HANG SEPARATELY!'

My late high school history teacher Paul Nagy at Norwalk High back in 1972-76 use to say to us;

"We have a terrible system of government, but it is better than All the rest!"

Let us labor then to keep Liberty alive through, in the words of Superman our boyhood hero,

"Truth, Justice, and the American Way."

THE SECRET TO WORLD PEACE

Jesus the great Teacher, Prophet, Rabbi, and I believe Messiah, taught His followers this from the Old Testament Shema. In the Gospel of Matthew 22:34-40, He is asked, 'What is the Greatest Commandment?' And He responds by quoting from Deuteronomy 6:5:

You shall love the LORD your God with all your heart...
soul... and mind... and you shall love your neighbor
as yourself.

Love God.

Love your neighbor.

There it is! There you have the Big Secret to world peace, which in its simplicity, is no secret at all. We only need to go back to the Ancient wisdom of Holy Scripture. As I often have told people as a pastor and priest; 'Read Your Bible and say Your Prayers!'

SALVATION PROMISE: Acts 16:31

Whosoever calls upon the Name of the LORD shall be saved!

I believe though to achieve World Peace, we must First find peace in our own hearts. And that starts finding Peace with God. I encourage the reader to open a Bible and search out these things for themselves. The Bible says in Romans 5:1, 'We can have peace with God' through a relationship with Jesus.

Now some will ask, 'How can I find God?' Whether you are in a fox hole, hospital bed, prison cell, on the sea, in the depths of the ocean, riding a cloud, or sitting in a cold quiet woods, or a hot searing dessert, GOD is there!

Read Psalm 139: HE wants you to know HE is with you! And HE loves you!

For God so loved the world, that He gave His One and only Son,
that whosoever believes in Him, will not perish but shall have
everlasting life!

St. John 3:16

This beautiful promise can be yours by merely asking God in a simple Prayer of Faith!

GOD Help me!

JESUS Save me!

LORD Forgive me!

HOLY SPIRIT I Believe!

SWEET JESUS, Have mercy on me...

It can be in your own words because God hears the prayer of every sincere and earnest heart.

That is why the Gospel is called *Good News,* in fact I believe, The Best News Ever!

Peace I leave with you; My peace I give unto you, not as the world gives... don't let your heart be troubled, neither let it be afraid.

St. John 14:37

I wish for you my friend, SHALOM!

Rev Johnny Cardamone

APPENDIX:
Future Editions: War Stories of the
21st Century: The War on Terror

Dear Veteran, Friend, & Family, January 24, 2020

This year marks the 75th anniversary of the end of WWII, which changed our country and our world forever. I remember being moved by President Ronald Reagan's stirring speech at Normandy in 1984, which inspired me to travel to Europe the following summer. And while painting my 90-year-old grandma Cardamone's living room on June 6th, 1994 I watched the 50th anniversary of D-Day. That is when the idea for collecting these stories came to me. I asked her to tell me some of the stories I remembered hearing as a boy, including those of my four uncles; stories about the Depression and the War years. Thus, began my desire of recording these stories for history. Shortly after this Tom Brokow came out with his best seller, "The Greatest Generation!" And that truly describes what these folks accomplished, in saving Western civilization from 20th century despots and tyranny.

Twenty-five years have now passed, and many others have shared this same vision. And many of these warriors are now gone. The history of what our fathers, grandfathers, brothers, uncles, cousins, mothers and friends accomplished, must be recorded and live on so that we never forget the bloody lessons of the four major wars of the 20th century, and the new conflicts of the 21st century; a generation which since 9/11 has been born, raised, and come of age in a time defined by the issues of global terrorism.

For this reason, we hope we have accomplished our three simple goals: First, to remember their history, and its lessons, for it has been said that those who forget the past are doomed to repeat it. We neglect this word of wisdom at our own peril. And secondly, to honor the sacrifices of so many who came before us to secure our freedoms. And finally, perhaps in some small way, we can help to prevent future wars, for it is said the first casualty of any war is TRUTH!

For these reasons we request your help in collecting stories of veterans and their families to be transcribed into a book preserving a written, audio, and even video record. If you would like to share your memories or that of a loved one, please contact me at the address below.

Thank you for your time, and may God bless you, our country, and all Freedom loving people everywhere on this earth!

Rev. Johnny Cardamone
Copyright June 6, 1994
    To Share Your Stories please contact us below @
    WAR STORIES & REMEMBRANCE
    P.O. Box 943 Norwalk, Connecticut 06856
    Office 203-838-0100 or
    E-mail: Revjohnnycardamone@gmail.com

SUGGESTED FORMAT OF INFORMATION:

This is only a suggestion to get the process of recording your thoughts and recollections to flow more easily. We want the story told in your own words, and especially the impact that war experiences played on shaping your life, your faith, and your family, our country, and the world in which we live.

NAME & ADDRESS: _____

PHONE: _____ E-MAIL: _____

AGE & DATE ENLISTED & BRANCH OF SERVICE: _____

_____

BASIC TRAINING: _____

THEATER OF OPERATIONS: _____

WAR STORIES & REMEMBRANCE:

INCLUDING BATTLE EXPERIENCES:

- ❖ GROWING UP: YOUR EARLY YEARS

- ❖ MOST MEMORABLE EXPERIENCES & FRIGHTENING SITUATIONS

- ❖ YOUR VIEW OF GOD & FAITH IN THE MIDST OF WAR

- ❖ HOW YOU WERE CHANGED BY YOUR EXPERIENCE?

- ❖ THE IMPACT ON YOUR FUTURE & CAREER, AND WHAT YOU DID FOLLOWING THE WAR

- ❖ SOME FUNNY MEMORIES

- ❖ YOUR VIEW ON THIS PRESENT GENERATION & OUR COUNTRY'S DIRECTION

- ❖ LIFE ON THE HOME FRONT

- ❖ OTHER ADDITIONAL THOUGHTS & FURTHER MEMO-RIES

(Please use additional paper or record your thoughts on email using this outline as a general guide)

PHOTO/VIDEO/AUDIO
CONSENT AND RELEASE FORM

I hereby give my consent and permission to WAR STORIES its affiliates and agents, to have these stories and any photos, videos, audio or supporting material associated with them, to be published as an historic record, and to the best of my recollection I certify the accuracy and authenticity of this content. I also understand that this constitutes no offer or agreement for remuneration, compensation, or royalties, now or in the future for the shared material. However, you will receive a complimentary copy once published.

SIGNED: NAME: X: _____

PRINTED NAME: _____

ADDRESS: _____

_____ DATE:_____

COMMENTS:_____

Please MAIL or EMAIL All responses to *WAR STORIES &*
REMEMBRANCE **to P.O. Box 943 Norwalk, Connecticut 06856 or**
E-mail: Revjohnnycardamone@gmail.com.

THANK YOU FOR YOUR HELP & MAY GOD BLESS YOU!

AUTHOR & EDITOR'S FINAL NOTE:

Every attempt has been made in good faith to recount, retell, and re-
late the accounts of these 'War Stories' with accuracy and clarity, cap-
turing as much as possible each individuals' words and sentiment.
Any necessary corrections or changes will be made in future editions
of this publication.

PRAY FOR OUR TROOPS!

Rev. Johnny Cardamone

Johnny grew up in Norwalk, Connecticut. He attended Norwalk Public Schools, continued his education at Norwalk Community College, received a B.A. from Florida Bible College in 1982, and went on to earn his M.Div. from Capital Bible Seminary in 1988.

Over the past three decades Johnny has traveled extensively. He's been to 25 countries, including spending time in Israel studying archeology & political studies at the University of Jerusalem, and a summer doing mission work in Central America.

Johnny also had four uncles who served in WWII, which is where his passion for history and the desire to honor the sacrifices of both soldiers and civilians began. *War Stories and Remembrance* is the first in a series he is authoring/compiling in their honor.

In addition to pastoring three churches in Fairfield County Connecticut, Johnny continues to pursue his ministry work.

Joy in Proclaiming Christ Ministries began in 2002. Its mission is to: *"Build Bridges through pastoral prayer partnerships across racial, ethnic, denominational and international boundaries to offer the good news of Jesus Christ."* Its vision is to: *Offer hope, help, & healing to hurting and oppressed people everywhere.*

Liberty News Publishing: Our goal is to share objective truths people can utilize to make informed decisions in the preservation of our precious freedoms.

Made in the USA
Middletown, DE
02 October 2021

49013542R00124